Adolphus Alfred Jack

Essays on the Novel as Illustrated by Scott and Miss Austen

Adolphus Alfred Jack

Essays on the Novel as illustrated by Scott and Miss Austen

ISBN/EAN: 9783337001650

Printed in Europe, USA, Canada, Australia, Japan

Cover: Foto ©Thomas Meinert / pixelio.de

More available books at **www.hansebooks.com**

Essays on the Novel

Essays on the Novel

AS ILLUSTRATED BY SCOTT AND
MISS AUSTEN

BY

ADOLPHUS ALFRED JACK

𝔏𝔬𝔫𝔡𝔬𝔫

MACMILLAN AND CO., LIMITED

NEW YORK : THE MACMILLAN COMPANY

1897

PREFACE

In a history of prose fiction which the author read many years ago, he remembers vividly a passage in which the advantages of a good title were extolled. For himself he is free to confess that he had difficulty in finding a title at once accurately setting forth the purport of the following pages, and of a printable length. The present work does not propose either to treat of the novel as a whole, or to furnish its readers with a minute critical account of Scott and Miss Austen. Every observer of the literature of the present day is aware that among the many tendencies to be seen at work in contemporary fiction, there is one especially noticeable, leading to the composition of tales in which the interest of the characters is frankly subordinated to that of the action; and many an observer must have asked how far the practice of the older novelists supported this tendency, and how far it militated against it. In his private speculations on this topic the author was led to ask himself: what is the true sphere of the novel? and, specifically, what in a novel are the true spheres of character and action? The outcome is this book in which Scott and Miss Austen are reviewed with an eye to these questions.

The discussion is timeworn, yet it is hoped that the treatment, as much the result of accidental circumstances as of any purely philosophical intention, may have some of the attraction of novelty. Another critic might have preferred to speak more at large, and to have brought under contribution all literature from Rome to Boston, or at least the whole literature of the English novel from Richardson to Thackeray. But apart from the natural difficulties inseparable from a task of such magnitude, there were two good reasons against so ambitious a course. The critic who in his study

and with time at his disposal, speaks of everything, will not find many readers with sufficient
learning or leisure to check his statements; and
since the size of volumes and the patience of the
public are equally limited, he who produces a
hundred examples must be reduced from mere
want of space to making many unsupported
assertions. These circumstances taken together,
the author inclined to speak only of a few
books, and of those minutely. He believed that
in the more familiar novels of Scott, and in
Miss Austen's little masterpieces, he had ample
material for his purpose. What he proposed to
himself was, firstly, to write an introductory
chapter, sketching very rapidly the history of
the novel in England; secondly, to treat Scott
as a novelist of character and action, with
especial reference to six novels that are on
every school-room shelf; and, thirdly, to deal
with Miss Austen generally, to show how a
writer who laid little stress on action, could
attain success, and what manner of success she
might attain. Besides this, it appeared proper

to state shortly, and by way of preface to a more detailed criticism, what was the general estimate of Scott on which that criticism was based.

This plan, with one exception, has been carried out. Any one who has ever written a book through which a thesis runs, knows how insistent its iteration is apt to appear, and how irresistible is the temptation to stray, to wander into alluring by-paths, and to discuss matters just seen from the high road. In these essays this temptation has not always been resisted. The reader perhaps may be disposed to quarrel with them because it has not been yielded to oftener for the purpose of supplying a more complete estimate of the writers discussed. There are already before the public a very considerable number of criticisms on both novelists; but the author would not take refuge in that, and he admits the danger that an essay on Scott in which only the most cursory reference is made to his humour may easily be misleading. He had, however, his reasons for the course he has adopted. To speak of that subject at length did not lie in his way. With Miss Austen it was different: her wit entered into the discussion ; without its aid her slight narratives would never have caught the general attention. Scott offers a large field for inquiry, and one may discuss how he has used action for its own sake, or for the elucidation of character without taking more than passing notice of his humorous figures. Indeed, it would have been difficult to have taken more notice of them without having lost all sight of the high road. A humorous character, unless he is as important as Falstaff, has singularly little to do; his is a speaking, not a walking part. Humour such as Scott and Shakespeare have is often but the overflow of the man, and one might write a treatise on Shakespeare's use of action without coming a whit nearer the explanation how he has made Shallow live.

The author, in conclusion, desires to acknowledge his obligations to those critics who, when he last appeared before them, spoke their minds with a candour which certainly ought to have had beneficial results. How far he has bene-

fited by the process it is fortunately not for him
to judge, nor has he much hope that the present volume, which is openly concerned with a
dogma built upon a number of subsidiary pronouncements, will escape the former charge of
dogmatism. He pleads guilty to a doubt in his
own mind whether, unless the critic of great
authors is to become the curious painter of
admiration marks, it is altogether possible for
him not to dogmatize. Everything cannot be
praised, nor can everything that cannot be
praised be neglected, for there is nothing more
likely to confuse our sense of proportion. The
great authors are not comparable with the reign-
ing sovereigns of the Middle Ages, who, it was
part of loyalty to suppose, could not err. They
leave their works as a kind of perpetual legacy,
which it is any one's privilege to handle and
assay. Unless we "touch and fear not" we shall
hardly get from them that standard of excellence of which each generation stands so much
in need, yet claims to have fitted to its altered
requirements. Criticism, at its best, is little

more, and surely it is no less than an evaporating series of dogmas representing the frank mood of the time or the individual in regard to masterpieces. The style of Hazlitt, who has already lived beyond the period commonly set to critical life, is a fusillade of brilliant assertions. Mr. Arnold, who did more for criticism than any Englishman of his generation, is never more himself than when emphasizing a provoking dictum. It is true that Hazlitt's wealth of ideas disguises the fact that he is dogmatizing, and Mr. Arnold's charm is such that we forget he is contradicting dogma. When therefore one hears it objected to a critic that he is dogmatic, one must suppose it to be meant that he has not grace to hide his dogmatism. This is a fault, certainly, which he may obviate if he can, but it is not the fault with which he is charged.

CONTENTS

ESSAYS ON THE NOVEL

THE NOVEL

NOW-A-DAYS, said Sir William Harcourt, every one is a Socialist. It is easy to form epigrams in this manner; all that is necessary being to select one of the numerous prevailing tendencies of the day, and to state the fact of its existence with sufficient emphasis. If it gives the politician comfort to repeat that every one is a socialist, the same kind of comfort is secured to the literary man by exclaiming that now-a-days every one is a novelist. The same kind of comfort is attained, as also the same degree of truth. If the socialist is a prominent element of our political life, the novelist in literature is equally conspicuous. Sir William Harcourt, when he coined his famous phrase, meant to silence the criticisms of those who were afraid

B

of the socialistic tendencies of the time, by assuring them that the vogue of socialism was no longer a coming event to be deplored, but a fact, however unpalatable, to be accepted, and there is no doubt that, to a large extent, with those whom he got to believe in him, he succeeded. In the field of practical politics criticism is silent before what is thought to be inevitable. It is the tendency of criticism everywhere, and if we can be induced to believe that a habit—whether that of the State regulation of property, or that of the composition of fictitious tales—is fixed, we care the less to inquire how that habit has been formed, or whether indeed, a still more essential question, it ought to have been formed at all. We have come to believe in the natural ascendency of the novel, and as a consequence to accept the fact of its ascendency, without inquiry or demur. As, however, a cursory acquaintance with the facts of the history of the novel in England will ensure the conviction that its modern ascendency is rather accidental than natural, and as its position relative to the drama to-day is fraught with consequence to the future of letters, justification will not be wanting when the inquirer presents himself.

Now-a-days every one is a novelist: it is a heightened way of stating what criticism has of late years iterated, that all our present creative literary talent goes to the making of novels. The last of the great poets whose names have adorned this century alone remains with us; occasionally in the last decade or two there has been produced a chamber drama of excellence, but in this time all the reputations that have been made or increased are, almost without exception, those of novelists. The drama, as an active influence, is given over to the study of social difficulties, or to the close imitation of contemporary life; it is no longer open, since our modern laws and ethics are by no means beautiful things, but, on the contrary, plain and uninspiring, as a field for the display of the poetical imagination. Even our fancies lead us into the immediate presence of the practical and useful, an arid imaginative atmosphere in which poetry has died of inanition. The drama, with its gaze concentrated on temporary improvements, and drawn away from actions of abiding interest, no longer fulfils its highest function of dealing with life at large. Poetry, lacking sustenance, has lost its vitality. Meanwhile all the imagination, all the artistic intelligence of the nation is devoted to the production of novels. The best work of recent years has been done in the novel, and in all probability there will be done in it the best work of the years immediately to come.

In this statement of the present position of affairs there will seem to some nothing surprising. Why should it not be so? they will ask, How should it be otherwise? The answer is, that it has generally not been so, that it has seldom not been otherwise. The present ascendency of the novel, an ascendency which I confess to thinking has not yet reached its height, is a development wholly modern, for so far is the novel from being the obviously best form for imaginative work, that nine-tenths of the great imaginative work of the world has been done in other forms.

Without entering on a question so open to dispute as that concerning the original virtue of mankind, it will be safe to premise that man in his origin is a truthful animal. Some degree of civilization, some touch of cultivation is necessary before the savage can rise to the conception of a lie: it is so much easier to tell the truth. So natural is it, indeed, that to state the thing

that is not is even in modern societies a matter
of some difficulty.   If I see a man running, and
I am asked shortly after whether I have seen
any one hastening away, my instinct is to answer
"Yes."   If I answer "No," it can only be that I
have some reason for not saying "Yes," perhaps
a desire to shield a fugitive friend, or some disinclination to serve the inquirer.   The members of
an early society, therefore, will narrate what they
have seen, and they will narrate only what they
have seen: it does not occur to them to do anything else.   In an early society a narrative of no
consequence will almost certainly be truthful.
Putting aside those, then, who in the exigencies
of daily life feel the pressure of a difficult occasion, or to put it less euphemistically, find a lie
occasionally convenient, the temptation to tamper
with the truth will obtrude itself first upon those
who deal with weighty affairs.   The poet and
the teller of sagas will be the first to feel it, since
it is they who are the narrators of heroic actions.
The poet who addresses himself to the task of
narrating truthfully—and this is the task to which
in early societies he does address himself—the
heroic lives of the ancestors of his race or the
myths, not myths to him, which detail the heroic

deeds of early gods, will soon encounter the difficulty that some of the actions of which he has heard are not heroic at all, or at least not sufficiently heroic for consistency with the rest. His temptation will be to exaggerate the less notable incidents, to heighten them, to bring them in line with the others; and this device, so characteristically poetical as to have obtained the name of poetic exaggeration, he, or his successors, will employ with increasing freedom till a large element of fiction has intruded itself within their work. The drama, a later development, and like the early sagas and epics, having its origin in historical or religious legends, will follow a similar course. At first the legend will be adhered to, but gradually more and more departed from, till at length the dramatic poet will deal without scruple with the avowedly fictitious. The saga and the drama will be the first to emancipate themselves from the despotism of fact.

It does not indeed follow of necessity that those efforts are in form poetical, there being nothing in the nature of a drama to compel its composition in verse, nor anything in that of the earliest traditional tales of a nation to prevent

their being occasionally written in prose. But
though those efforts are not necessarily poetical
in form, yet that they generally are so is but a
consequence from the fact that their material is
always poetical material. It is the kind of
material that ought properly, and will certainly in
time come to be narrated in verse. As a matter
of fact, it may not always happen that the
earliest compositions into which a large element
of the fictitious enters are metrical, nevertheless
they are either poetry or productions tending to
become poetry ; they are the children of the
poetical imagination. Imagination then finds
its natural outlet in following the course of
poetry, and, in following the course of poetry, it
proceeds to shape the material into accordance
with its requirements, till there is finally evolved
the imaginative drama.

Long before the modern imaginative drama
was at its height, prose had been taking, more
and more, the licence of fiction. The desire for
stories had grown till the story-teller, finding his
heroic legends exhausted, was driven to seek
new subjects among the occurrences of familiar
life, where the call upon fiction to supplement his
material was more imperative. But though this

development cannot be neglected by the student who wishes to study in detail the history of the drama, it is still a late development: it is, so to speak, an unnatural development, a development of exhaustion. The imagination, first exercised on poetical subjects, following its natural development, will develop itself poetically, and so much is this so that when the novel first appears as a mature growth in modern Europe, in the tales of Boccaccio and his school, it is caught up at once, and its imaginative possibilities carried out by the poets and dramatists. On those tales, many of them only partly, but some of them wholly fictitious, the Elizabethan dramatists seized, and exercised their imagination upon them in much the same way as the classic poets did with the old legends of their particular countries. And though this is only an instance, it would be difficult to find any serious exception to the general rule that the imagination of all countries found not only its first, but its easiest development in poetry and the drama.

As one might have expected, the first efforts of English fictitious prose are to be found in the historical or legendary romance, that is to say, in England, long before any one thought of composing a false and familiar tale, the imagination, when it was not at work with poetry or metrical composition, was at work with poetical material. Almost all these early English romances—the qualification is introduced to meet the exceptions which modern scholarship is so quick to furnish to every general statement—have a historical or legendary basis. The greatest of them, the 'Morte d'Arthur,' derived like most of the others from continental sources, is no exception to the rule. In a strict sense it is no more a fictitious tale than the 'Iliad' or the 'Aeneid.' It professes to tell the truth, but it does not profess to be bound by it. To the central incidents, already familiar to a multitude of people in Brittany and England, those responsible for its production do not confine themselves. On the contrary, we are furnished with the sayings of the characters, matter of necessity purely imaginary, and also with a number of trivial details which the spoken word could not preserve. To the 'Morte d'Arthur' the term novel is totally inapplicable; the 'Morte d'Arthur' is no more a novel than the 'Odyssey' is a novel; it is a prose epic, indulging, perhaps from its being written in prose, perhaps from the idiosyncrasy of the peoples among whom it took form, rather more freely in what was known to be fictitious detail than was common with classical epic poetry.

'Euphues,' the next outstanding work in the history of English prose fiction, is a composition of another kind, and for the explanation of its appearance attention must be directed to other influences, to those excited by Boccaccio's tales and the 'Gesta Romanorum.' With the gist of some of the former, Chaucer, before the publication of Malory's book, had already made English readers familiar. About fifty years after its publication, many of them were translated directly by Painter and others. To the influence of the latter 'Euphues' perhaps owes as much, owes as much at least as regards the habit of mind which was responsible for its production. The monks in their sermons having to provide, as all moralists have had to provide, against dulness, struck upon the notion of speaking in entertaining and contemporary parables to which an explanation was appended. In the 'Gesta Romanorum,' a collection of these monkish sermons, this idea of inventing a number of idle tales "for our doctryne," as they would have expressed it, took literary form.

As a result, though the entertainment of the story was often more obvious than its application, and invariably of far greater length, the fancy of the Middle Ages was caught. In the interests, or in what by each successive generation have been thought to be the interests of morality, much has been pardoned, and many strange courses adopted, and in the interests of morality the first English novel was written. It says, however, a great deal for the original strangeness of this particular medium in which imagination was to exercise itself so freely, that long after the licence of artistic invention had been granted to the poet, it was still unclaimed by the writer in sober prose. So much was this so that it is doubtful if even Lyly, the first English novelist, would have thought of writing a story for the mere sake of telling it. In 'Euphues' the sole use of the adventure was to ensure the perusal of the treatise; its first aim was didactic. 'Euphues, the Anatomy of Wit,' published in 1579, has the distinction of being the first of a long series of productions of which it was in no sense intended to be one: Lyly wrote the first English novel without intending to write a novel: the first English novel appears as the fringe of an educational treatise.

Sir Philip Sidney's 'Arcadia,' on the other hand, has no didactic intention; in it the fictitious story or rather series of stories seeks no other justification than that afforded by the interest of the events. There were two reasons for this difference. In the first place many of the incidents in the 'Arcadia' are those of the older legends, and in England, for the refurbishing of old legends there needed, by this time, no excuse. It had become a customary, as it was in some sort a poetical thing, to relate with a certain amount of freedom these half historical and essentially poetical tales. In the second place Sidney as a prose writer considered himself entitled to the licence of a poet. "Like almost all of his contemporaries," says Mr. Raleigh in his interesting work on the English novel, "Sidney defined poetry so as to include any literary work of the imagination, and absolutely refused to make of rhyming or versing an essential;" and again, "the characteristics of Sidney's style are in a large measure attributable to his conception of the 'Arcadia' as a 'prose poem.'" And so, it may be added, are the general characteristics of the work. It seemed almost as natural for Sidney in his prose poem to give the rein to his imagination, as for a poet to write poetry on an imaginative subject. Poetry, then, which had long enjoyed the licence of fiction, presided at the birth of the second considerable English novel, just as morality which had long derived support from fiction presided at the birth of the first.

No doubt, if one were to use terms with absolute precision the name novel might be denied to both; a novel, as we understand the term now, being a fictitious story dealing with familiar events,—events, that is, taking place in an ordinary and not in a legendary or mythical world, and dealing with them with no other than an artistic object. Lyly's tale had another object, while Sidney's tale, far from dealing wholly with familiar, dealt in some part with legendary, and in great part with chivalric events. But whether we grant the name or withhold it, for our present purpose it is sufficient that in 'Euphues' and the 'Arcadia,' we have two stories, avowedly fictitious, dealing with familiar events, and written in prose, and that Greene, Nash and Lodge, all contemporaries

of Sidney, all produced short compositions,
certain of which fulfil every requirement of the
novel. Of these writers, Lodge was the only
one who, as far as is known, consistently wrote
stories without any ulterior purpose, though
even he is suspected of an occasional auto-
biographical intention. Greene dipped into
autobiography, and more than dipped into
didactics. Nash wrote only one novel, the rest
of his imaginary and familiar scenes occurring
in controversial pamphlets. Nevertheless the
novel had arrived. One can say no more
indeed ; it had come with difficulty, and it had
not come to stay. The novel had arrived ; but
the drama, affording a more natural field for
the exercise of the imagination, was just at its
zenith, and to the construction of dramas, during
the remainder of Elizabeth's, and the whole of
James's reign, the imagination of the country
went.

With the gradual decline of the drama the
novel reappeared, and this time again as an
importation from abroad. The form in which
it returned was not auspicious. In France it
had become the custom to select some character
or characters of classic times, and to build

around them a huge series of imaginary adventures. The custom was copied in England, and thus we find the English fictitious tale, half-a-century after its comparatively mature development in the hands of Nash, again in close connection with fact. In the whole curious history of the English novel, there is nothing more curious than this doubling back on its course. The novelists of this new movement are found inventing legends to tack on to a historical character, making, as it were, a kind of fictitious history, just as the old writers were found inventing characters to fill out a legend. The novelist had been laboriously evolved from the imaginative narrator of real legends, only to become the narrator of legends purely imaginary. The public had been told what were in the main believed to be the facts about characters whom many deemed mythical; the business to which the seventeenth century romancists applied themselves was that of telling what no one believed or was expected to believe about characters known to be historical. In a word, the old legends were exhausted, and these romancists of a later day imagined new. In a scheme of this sort, it is

easy to see, there was no lasting vitality. The
immense multitude of these romances produced
would by itself convince us that in their time
they enjoyed a considerable reputation, but with
their time their reputation ended, and they died,
as the heralds say of childless men, *sine prole*.
At the moment of their decease there was
nothing ready to take their place, and the novel,
defeated in its attempt to show that an imaginative tale is best told in interminable prose, fell
back into temporary obscurity. Our modern
novel took its rise not in the desire to tell a
story, but in the desire to draw a character.

" The works of the lesser writers of the seventeenth century," says Mr. Raleigh, "show the
rise of a new spirit, foreign to the times of
Shakespeare,—a spirit of observation, of attention to detail, of stress laid upon matter of fact,
of bold analysis of feeling, and free argument
upon institutions; the microscope of the men
of the Restoration, as it were, laying bare the
details of daily objects, and superseding the
telescope of the Elizabethans that brought the
heavens nearer earth. No one word will finally
describe it; in its relation to knowledge it is
the spirit of science, to literature it is the spirit

of criticism." The prose of the latter part of the seventeenth century directed itself to the study of subjects with which prose is peculiarly competent to deal: it gave itself to the work of observation and criticism. As the offspring of this tendency there sprung from the press a number of "characters," short essays on the characteristics of types, some diaries enlisting the interest of the public in matters of familiar concern, and a whole literature of essays in which every corner of the social state was brought under review. A minute study of man, and his habits of thought and conduct, became the real business of letters. To bring vividly before his fellows the movements of a mind subjected to religious impressions, Bunyan wrote his famous story of 'The Pilgrim's Progress.' To illustrate the characteristics of a genuine English squire Addison wrote various chapters of a disconnected novel on the life of Sir Roger de Coverley. Questions the most diverse concerning human nature and government, came to be asked, and answers to them were attempted in a series of hypothetical cases. There is a correspondence too interesting to escape notice, between these first considerable

efforts of the English novel, and the serious
essays on the relations of the sexes, and the
proper position of woman, which to-day take
the form of fiction ; nor must the abuse which
honesty often provokes, induce the critic to
forget that what the more earnest of a growing
school are doing, is just that which was done
so successfully at the beginning of last century.
How would man comport himself in solitude ?
asked Defoe,—for the fact of Alexander Selkirk's
imprisonment had by itself no absorbing artistic
interest,—and immediately there came from his
pen a novel, and not, as would have happened
fifty years before, a speculative discussion. What
is man like ? asked Swift, and his answer is
to be found in 'Gulliver's Travels.' In all these
cases there is a story, but to get the attitude of
the time we must remember that it is not there
for itself. Matters are similar with Richardson ;
his incident is subsidiary to his main purpose,
and though his novels have a narrative, they
are studies of character. "If you were to read
Richardson for the story," said Johnson, and
the remark is as true as it is famous, "your
impatience would be so much fretted that you
would hang yourself. But you must read

him for the sentiment, and consider the story only as giving occasion for the sentiment,"—testimony, and contemporary testimony too, that the first great English novelist was in touch with the influences which brought the English novel about. Nor were his great and immediate successors, though far more attentive to the interest of the narrative, in the habit of treating it as of paramount importance. With these writers—and Fielding, despite Coleridge's puzzling remark that the plot of 'Tom Jones' is one of the three best in the world, does not seem to be an exception—we have to consider the story but as a series of incidents giving opportunity to the characters. The story of 'Tom Jones' itself, which cannot be denied to be admirably suited for its purpose, is little else, and if Coleridge meant what it is just possible he did mean, that the plot of 'Tom Jones' was as admirably adapted to the requirements of the novel as those of 'The Oedipus Tyrannus' and 'The Alchemist' to the requirements of the drama, there will be few to disagree. The novel, it cannot be too plainly stated, in the hands of Richardson, Fielding, Sterne, Smollett and Goldsmith, was a patient study of familiar character

and emotion.   In their hands the novel, for the
first time in England, was seriously set to do
work which was not distinctively poetical, work
too minute and too unimaginative for poetry to
do.   It was not long, however, before the novel
again betook itself to imaginative subjects, and
again attempted to secure attention for the
interest of the story alone.   Horace Walpole,
Mrs. Radcliffe, M. G. Lewis, and even Godwin—
when we leave 'Caleb Williams' with its political
intention out of account,—all wrote tales depending for their effect upon the imaginative
nature of the incidents.   The interest excited
by the persons introduced was strictly secondary.
As far as characters were drawn, they were
drawn, not with the loving detail of Fielding or
Goldsmith, but only in their general aspect.

To both these schools, the school of character
distinguished by many famous names, and the
school of incident with its long, and, up to
Scott's day, comparatively inglorious record, the
Waverley novels owe something.   On the one
hand, as in 'The Antiquary,' we have studies of
character pure and simple, on the other imaginative stories like 'The Bride of Lammermoor,'
while between them there is a long series of

tales like 'Old Mortality,' which, though depending for part of their interest on dramatic incidents, contain studies of character as careful
as anything to be found where the interest of
the narrative is purely subordinate. In contra-
distinction to Scott, Miss Austen pays allegiance
entirely to the school of character. Working in
a smaller field than any of her great predecessors,
she is also far more indifferent than any of them,
to the rule which prescribes that before individuals will display the deeper side of their
natures they must be cast among large events.
To come to later times, with Thackeray and
Dickens and George Eliot, the novel is mainly
a study of character; with our actual contemporaries too often a fictitious tale. It is a
history full of interest. Prose fiction on its first
appearance in England was occupied, when
differences of temper and circumstances are
taken into consideration, in doing much the
same work, which in a minor, if also in a whole-
hearted way it is doing at the present time. No
modern novelist would venture into a world of
dragons, knights, and shepherdesses, or even
into one of magic mirrors, halls of Eblis, and
enchanted casques. That world for all prose

purposes is altogether dead. But strangely enough the modern counterpart of it, a world of adventurers and heightened adventures, is found much more easily than the modern counterpart of the world of Richardson and Fielding. The collocation of ideas may seem grotesque, but ‘Treasure Island,’ the parent of a lively progeny, may fairly be taken as our modern equivalent for the old prose tales of chivalry and romance. Probably, in this exaggerated form, of purely temporary duration, the development is still surprising. It took the novel, as a medium in which an imaginative story might be told, nearly two hundred years to gain a footing in England. The novel of character, if we except its easily explainable failure in the Elizabethan period, had only to appear to be accepted. Was it an accident that it so fell out, or are these historical facts a testimony to the genius of the novel which novelists cannot safely neglect? To attempt an explanation of them is to attempt an answer to the question.

The success of the novel of character is the more easily explained. In the first place, it must be apparent that there are certain things

which poetry cannot do, or can do only in a lame and perfunctory manner. Poetry is at a disadvantage when any realistic effort is attempted, the poetical imagination, whether using the form of verse or the form of prose, being just that faculty by which we rise above the details of ordinary life. Poetry, with the swift methods incidental to the art, is little fitted to analyze the petty variations of ordinary character, and if life in all its aspects is to be submitted to close observation and intricate criticism, the office must be performed by prose. In the second place, when Richardson began to write, there was a widespread desire among the educated class to submit life to this process of observation and criticism. The only reason why the novel of character did not succeed before the eighteenth century, was that before the eighteenth century no such general desire had existed. The true reason why the novel of character has had so long and so successful a history in modern times is, that since the eighteenth century such a desire has continued to exist. The success of the novel of character may be explained at once by saying that the form was better suited than any other for doing the work to which it was set. Slowly as the taste for prose fiction has arisen, the taste must remain as long as there is a desire for a kind of work which nothing but prose fiction can perform. It is not a poetical work, and therefore prose is necessary; the interest of the reader must be sustained for a considerable period in imaginary events, without the proper manipulation of which character cannot be properly displayed, and therefore some kind of story is essential.

To explain the failure of the novel of incident is more troublesome. But to turn first to the facts—the history of the novel of incident shows conclusively, what indeed may be shown in other ways, that poetry is the most natural medium for imaginative work, that the imagination first exercises itself in poetry or on poetical material. And as a kind of corollary to this, the history of the novel of incident shows conclusively that it was a work of immense difficulty to accustom the public to an essentially prose narrative of imaginary events. Few, for instance, would have thought of asking Chaucer why he told stories in verse; almost every one would have been a little surprised had the educational object

of Lyly's 'Euphues' not been apparent on its
face. It seemed natural for the poet to imagine
occurrences, it did not seem natural for events
to be imagined in sober prose; it did not seem
natural, nor was there any sufficient reason why
a departure should be made from the ordinary
course. Had the novel of character not taken
root in England, it is doubtful whether the novel
of incident would ever have been thought to
have justified its existence. Several times it
had attempted to gain a position on its own
merits, and several times it had failed; its
opportunity came, by a curious turn of literary
history, when the novel of character had established itself, and its success such as it is followed
in the train of the substantial successes achieved
by its rival. It was perhaps natural that it
should. A novel of character exists for the
delineation of the niceties of character and
emotion, but since it is a novel it must contain
incident, and it will happen occasionally that
undue emphasis is laid upon the action.
Habituated to these tales in prose, and forgetting
their original purpose, the reader will come to
take delight in the story itself, and from the
mere force of habit to accept unquestioningly

the form in which it is cast. The novel of
character, having a totally different intention
from the drama, and doing a totally different
work, drew, at least during the day's of its preponderating popularity, men's interest away
from dramatic events. And when interest in
regard to them reasserted itself, the novel of
character, changing with the tendency, was
replaced by a transition the most natural by the
novel of incident. The drama in modern times
has consequently what it never had before, a
competitor in the field. The novel of incident,
trading upon the taste formed by the novel of
character, satisfies also that other taste which
without it would have had to depend upon
poetical satisfaction. It is sufficiently remarkable that it should do this, since the novel of
incident, judged by itself, is little more than the
drama grown garrulous. Had it needed to win
acceptance on its own merits, it could never have
hoped to compete with it. It is true of course
that it is only in its nobler form, in ' The Bride
of Lammermoor ' for instance, that the novel
of incident can be so spoken of. In its more
familiar form there is nothing more unlike the
drama. There the only reasonable comparison,

when it does happen to appeal to the poetical emotions, is either with the Idyll, or with poems in ballad form. But there also, when it makes no kind of appeal to the poetical emotions, but confines itself to the narration of petty and prosaic details, it is, as its admirers point out with truth, a department of literary activity entirely modern and singular. This indeed is but another way of saying that for her long neglect of the novel of incident, history has more than a show of justification, since in its greater forms the novel of incident has encroached upon the province of poetry, and it is only in its less important that it has done work peculiar to itself.

The case of most interest is that in which the novel of incident joins issue with the drama, and for the purpose of glancing at that, it will be sufficient to take the instance already given, in all probability the one which would be selected by those who wished to establish the claims of the novel of incident as a separate literary form. ' The Bride of Lammermoor,' of all Scott's contributions to imaginative literature perhaps the greatest, has a host of excellences and scarcely a fault : the incidents are few, and extremely striking; the dialogue is often not only of poetical merit, but of the highest poetical merit; in the serious parts of the tale there is hardly a word wasted. But these excellences, it is important to notice, are the peculiar excellences of the drama—a great action, a serious and poetical dialogue, a total absence of verbiage,—and admirably as Scott tells his tale, it is impossible not constantly to feel that something is amiss. The speeches of the Master of Ravenswood, for example, come oddly in the midst of a narrative. They are so far removed from real life, so much the product of a heated brain, that, to lend them a full belief, we need to have brought before us, by the short clear methods of the drama, the actual scene which provoked them : in such cases nothing should come between the reader and the imaginary figures. Who would lend credit to the dialogue between Iago and Othello had Shakespeare furnished it with a running commentary in prose : who would not lose the illusion : who would not feel the discrepancy between the placid narrator and the creatures of his fancy? This is the danger which the prose narrator of such matters has to face. The dramatist, not having to narrate, escapes it, while the narrative poet avoids the difficulty by rising with his narrative, and though it is true that Scott in 'The Bride of Lammermoor' is continually and successfully doing what the poet does as a matter of course, it is done with effort. A prose narrative, however often it may attain to poetical excellence, can never have poetical excellence in the same degree as a poetical narrative, much less can a prose narrative, however often it may attain to dramatic excellence, possess the dramatic excellences of the drama. The great qualities of 'The Bride of Lammermoor,' it is difficult for any reader not to feel it, would have been still more evident had the story been told in dramatic form, while such faults as it has, an occasional excess of description, and the undue importance, detrimental to the tragic effect, which Scott has given to the character of Caleb, a dramatist would not have been tempted to commit. And if it is true that 'The Bride of Lammermoor' would have gained by being cast in dramatic form, it is evidently true of all of its successors, where the authors have not found it possible to overcome in the same degree the difficulties incidental to their task, where the narrative form has tempted them into prolixity, and prevented them from attaining, as Scott has attained, success.

But the excellence of the drama is not merely this, that it is the best medium for noble imaginative work, but also that it is a medium extremely ill-suited for the treatment of ignoble affairs. The drama, delighting in swift methods and great actions, does not readily suffer the interminable detail with which the realistic novel has made us familiar. The drama, when it becomes a drama of every-day incident—and how many of our modern dramas are no more—is seen to labour in its course. And though this want of adaptability on the part of the drama is just that which the partisans of the novel, an infinitely more flexible form, emphasize as its radical defect, I prefer to think of this, its distinguishing characteristic, as a real and salutary merit. The work which is peculiar to the novel of incident, and which it is able to do, as is proclaimed by those who are in touch with modern novels and modern dramas, far better than the drama, is work, of which in a modern society it is easy to have too much. In a modern society, the danger is not that our interest will be carried away from the affairs of

daily life, but that, on the contrary, we shall
cease to take interest in anything else, that our
imaginations will become stagnant, and that
ultimately we shall lose ourselves in idle wonder
at the variety of the commonplace. And in the
face of this tendency, it would perhaps not be
unreasonable to hope that on the literature of
the present day the novel of incident will come
to exercise a decreasing influence, since in its
virtual absence the imagination, dealing with
events rather for their own sake than for the
elucidation of character, would have to resort to
poetry, while the drama, freed from the competition of the novel of incident, would turn to
the work that was most natural to it. The
novel, doubtless, would remain with us, but it
would remain with an altered intention. However wide its range, it would have for its primary
object the study of character; however wide its
range—and its range would of necessity be wide
—we should get rid, at a stroke, of a whole
literature, that intolerable array of volumes in
which event is crowded upon event without
dignity or purpose. Whatever was peculiar to
the novel of incident, its series of artfully concocted improbabilities, its appeal to a jaded

fancy, its truthfulness where truth is trivial, would disappear, while whatever was excellent would be caught up and retained, that part, where the events, though familiar, were useful as machinery for developing character, by the more serious novel which would take its place, and that part where the events were important, by a drama which directed its gaze to subjects of poetical weight. The taste which the increasing production of these " light tales " has encouraged would die with them. The novel of incident took so long to come into being that it would not without difficulty be revived, and in this happy future, we should ask only of a character if it was interesting, and of an action if it was great.

CHAPTER I

SCOTT

IN this age of biography, when no sooner is a man of any eminence dead, than his family, his relatives, or his friends clamour for the story of his life, it is common to hear biographers complaining of the dearth of material. Of those complaints, the loudest and most just come from the biographers of literary men. In most instances their self-imposed task is a hard one. Every year, from different points of the compass, a certain number of youths go to London, and, once arrived there, spend existences of average duration in writing, as the case may be, a small or a great number of books. About the lives of such people there is a sameness which it is impossible for the biographer to get over. In the life of the ordinary literary man, there are, speaking generally, no events,

D

no excitements greater than those produced by
the reviews of meritorious books, and no periods
of great enthusiasm. The ordinary literary man
not only lives the ordinary life of the educated
classes, but his whole being is in touch with
them. He is one of a hundred thousand or two
who share his feelings, and, from the accident
that he spends his time in writing better than
his neighbours, one of a thousand similarly
occupied.

With the great authors there is this difference,
that though the path laid down for them is, in
most cases, that of the ordinary literary man,
they are so distinguished from their fellows, they
have so much of the fire that quickens, so eager
an interest in what passes through the mind,
that it seldom happens that their life is ordinary.
Let the circumstances in which they are placed
be as colourless as they may, something of their
own vitality will somewhere give it colour.
Even if the life is such as Wordsworth's, that
of the typical student or recluse, the greater
energy of the man will prevent it from becoming
merely typical, it will stand out from among
similar lives with a certain force of its own.
And just as wherever there is force and the

motion generated by it, wherever there is really
life, there is variety, so about the lives of the
great authors, however similar their circumstances, there is no sameness. Wordsworth,
Coleridge, Shelley, Keats, to mention only a
few, and those contemporaries of Scott, were all
men who spent their time in writing, yet how
different are the records of their days! So
distinct were their characters that even in the
limited possibilities of the literary career, the
individuality of each appears plainly, and it
is this that gives its fascination to literary
biography, a perpetual sameness of subject and
a perpetual difference of result.

The lives of the great authors all have interest;
it does not always happen that they also contain instruction. The force that makes whatever
they do remarkable drives them often into
excess; if not always an excess to be avoided,
at least one which cannot be imitated, and if
not useful as a warning certainly useless as an
example. If we wish to read for the purpose of
intelligent imitation, it is to 'Plutarch's Lives'
that we turn. Plutarch's soldiers and captains
were not men of imagination: what they saw,
other men see though not so clearly, and what

they did other men are continually doing on a
scale reduced. Those robust masters of an active
world astonish us not as the Laputans astonished
Gulliver, but as Gulliver astonished Lilliput.
The poet, the novelist, he who plays with ideas
is built of other stuff; he is distinguished from
us by his difference as well as by his greatness,
and his life is far less likely to serve for a model.
Nevertheless, there have been such lives; the
life of Wordsworth was such—and such, in all
essentials, was the life of Scott. Of the two,
Wordsworth's was the more blameless, the more
free from conventionality, and the more in consonance with a rigid individual ideal. However,
it was less human, and had less of dramatic
interest. Scott's very weaknesses—with one
exception, his punctilious severity in regard to
any departure from the code of chivalric honour
—all amiable, serve but to endear him to us,
and his life, in which great prosperity was
followed by great misfortune, has of necessity
more attraction than Wordsworth's, interesting
though Wordsworth's is, with the interest that
belongs to the actions of any one who sets
himself to climb the hill Difficulty. Great as
was Wordsworth's self-command, and much

reason as we have to believe that he would have come through any ordeal untouched, he was never subjected to so trying an ordeal as Scott. Scott's life has this supreme attraction for us, that, by the accident of events, he was submitted to the test.

Of the circumstances of his origin there is little that need here be said. Genius, an inexplicable thing, finds in Scott's case, as in others, only a trifling explanation in the history of his ancestors. One sees, of course, some indications there. From his mother, a lady with a taste for books, and the daughter of an Edinburgh professor, he may be thought to have inherited a literary inclination; while his father, a Writer to the Signet, and the descendant of an old border family at the head of which stand the Dukes of Buccleuch, may pass as sponsor at once for his martial instincts, and for that "thread of the attorney" which he playfully confessed to be in him. The child is not always the father of great men. With those whose minds are unreceptive the natural inclination counts for much, for less with those to whom experience is continually bringing new thoughts and supplying an amplifying corrective to the tendencies of youth. The most notable feature in Scott's childhood is the fortunate circumstance—a childish illness which left its trace in a lameness of the right leg—that sent him early to country scenes and open air. At his grandfather's farm at Sandy-Knowe, the locality of which is marked by the neighbouring ruin of Smailholm Tower, he laid the strong foundations of bodily and mental health. Smailholm, the mere relic of a border peel, is situated about a couple of miles from the road between Melrose and Dryburgh, where it passes Bemerside, the ancestral home of the Haigs, about whom the Rhymer's prophecy was written, and by a fiction kept fulfilled. Not an hour's walk from Smailholm, the Tweed, a few hundred feet below the highway, takes a bend of singular grace, and the tourist gazing from the spot at the turn of the road, where in after years Scott often drew rein to gaze at the most beautiful view in the lowlands, sees before him the broad river winding through a champaign country rich in hollow and wood and field, and guarded in the distance by low lines of faint blue hills. Not an hour's walk in the opposite direction lies the romantic ruin of Dryburgh Abbey, in

which Scott ultimately found a resting-place as
appropriate as Wordsworth's at Grasmere. A
morning's ramble will take a good walker from
Smailholm to Melrose, and thence following the
sweep of the Tweed, or, if he prefers it, by
Bowden Moor, in either case skirting the sudden
mass of the Eildon hills, to Selkirk, perched on
a small acclivity and looking over the valleys
of Ettrick and Yarrow. It would have been
difficult to have found a spot, in which the future
poet of the borderland could more suitably have
passed the plastic period of childhood.

At the age of seven Scott was sent to Edinburgh High School, leaving it when twelve years
old to enter Edinburgh University. That as a
boy he did not distinguish himself in the precise
studies of school and college, is no exception to
the rule with imaginative authors. Boys are
taught little but fact, since most boys, though
they may have the desire, have not the capacity
to deal with theory, and facts and an imaginative temperament are not readily reconciled.
While more ordinary students were occupying
themselves with the subjects of the schools,
Shelley was amusing himself with chemistry and
metaphysics, Coleridge with political discussions,

Wordsworth with his own meditations, and Scott with whatever books took his fancy. Leaving college at the early age of sixteen, he was apprenticed to a conveyancer, and became finally associated with the law in the character of an advocate in 1792. For the next ten years he pursued a variety of occupations, that of the law with tolerable assiduity, and considering his assiduity with success, that of a captain of yeomanry, and that of a collector of ballads. Besides this in these ten years he wrote something of his own, formed an unsuccessful attachment to a lady who became the wife of Sir William Forbes, and within a year after her marriage engaged himself to his future wife, Miss Charpentier. From the little evidence which we have on this subject it is, I think, clear that Scott considered himself in some degree ill-treated by his first love, and that the wound remained with him long. It is difficult to avoid seeing in the precipitation which characterized his engagement something which has the appearance of pride or pique, nor was his subsequent married life such as to warrant us in rejecting the inference. " At the distance of sixty years since and more," says Mr. Palgrave, whose name is a guarantee that the judgment is not a harsh one, "it may be allowable to add that although attended by considerable happiness, faithful attachment on his wife's part, and much that gave a charm to life, this marriage does not appear to have satisfied the poet's inner nature." It was characteristic of Scott that he should have extracted all its good from this union, rather than have wasted days in regretting that it did not reach his ideal.

From the publication of 'The Border Minstrelsy' in 1802 we may date the beginning of his poetical career. In the twelve years which followed he gave to a delighted world his long series of verse romances. Meanwhile, prospering in his work as a lawyer, he was appointed Sheriff of Selkirkshire in 1804, and taking up his abode, as was part of his duty, in that county, remained there at the delightful house of Ashestiel till his appointment to a clerkship of Session eight years later. In this period, nothing is more surprising than his literary activity. No doubt in actual output the period of the Waverley Novels was, if not more fertile, equally so; but by that time his work as a lawyer had become less serious, his attention, confined to the working out of one imaginative vein, was less distracted,

and continual toil had become a matter of
course. In those first twelve years he was new
to the life of application, which his unremitting
energy necessitated, and, taking up any literary
work that came to his hand, he could not always
find his task congenial. Fresh from his business
in the Sheriff-court or as an advocate, he turned
to editing Lord Somers' Tracts, or Sir Ralph
Sadler's State Papers, to supervising and furnish-
ing with adequate biographies the small libraries
of prose and verse Dryden and Swift have left,
or to reviewing at length the newest publications
of the day. Altogether, from 1802 to 1814, there
appeared with his name on the title-page, as
editor or author, nearly seventy volumes. The
industry of lawyers is famous, but this was the
fruit of a lawyer's leisure, and of a lawyer who
also found opportunity to write thirty thousand
lines of verse. Poetry of all the arts demands
the most single and devoted adherence, and
here is a poet flinging off a series of long
poems, which have never been ranked low, and
which still afford to a multitude some of the
happiest moments of their lives, in the intervals
of business sufficient for two, and those not
merely ordinary men.

On his removal from Ashestiel, Scott settled at Abbotsford, a few miles further down the Tweed, and it was there that he proceeded to build, with the profits of continual activity, and increasing popularity, the house that from the beginning to the end, as well in its furnishings as in its general outline, was the creation of its owner. I suppose he was the first poet who ever built a house; poets, not because they are wise, but because they are poor, having generally been content to live in buildings which the money of others has erected. Every one is aware how dearly he paid for his breach of this long-established custom, and every one who has visited Abbotsford must, I think, confess to a doubt whether the return even in stone and mortar was reasonably adequate. The house, always interesting for its associations, is in itself disappointing. Even the situation, in a country where at every turn one has glimpses of river and mountain, has few claims to praise. On one side the ground dips from the road to the entrance, while on the other little can be seen from the windows except the broad sweep of the Tweed, a long lumpish hill rising from its farther side, and shutting off the prospect. The

surrounding park, more suitable for a cottage
ornée than a mansion, gives the same impression
of want of space, and the rooms, with the single
exception of the library, which undoubtedly has
architectural beauty, are just such rooms as may
be found in any town-house of moderate size.
In the Castle of Lirias to which Gil Blas retired,
the rooms were perhaps no bigger, but then the
Castle of Lirias made no pretence of being large.
It is the fault of Abbotsford that it does; the
walls being built as solidly as the walls of a
palace or a fortress designed to resist attack.
The armoury, crowded with weapons of historic
interest, is but a tiny apartment, while Scott's
study, in essence the plain room of a workman
with an eye to his work, is surrounded by heavy
bookcases, with an iron gallery attached, and
effecting no greater convenience of reference than
could have been got by standing on a chair.
Instead of the feudal castle which Scott, rich as
for a literary man he was, never had the money
to build, we have a miniature imitation not
without antiquarian charm, but heavy, and con-
fessing at every corner that the desires of the
builder soared beyond his means. Abbotsford
has been selected to point the moral of many

tales, designed to show that we ought not to desire a settled habitation, wherein our children's children may live.   Had the house been plainer it is probable that an ambition so laudable and universal would have escaped the censure of those who forget the pointed saying in Ecclesiastes—"Wisdom is good together with an inheritance, and profitable unto them that see the sun."

Shortly after his removal to Abbotsford Scott struck the imaginative vein, which was to yield him not only fortune, but the larger and more enduring part of his renown.   One day in 1814, while rummaging among his papers at his house in Castle Street, Edinburgh, he came upon the fragment of a novel which he had begun in 1805 and then laid aside.   This was the first seven chapters of 'Waverley,' and, taking it up again, he finished the first of the Waverley Novels in three weeks.   A rough computation establishes the fact that had he continued producing at this extraordinary speed he would have completed the whole series in less than three years.   Such a task was beyond the powers of a mortal, but the calculation has interest as showing the manner of his working, the determination with which he addressed himself to any given employment, and the power of his magnificent faculties when thoroughly aroused. To the production of novels these faculties were now to be chiefly directed, though it was still as always his habit to seek relaxation, with him but another name for change of occupation, in the lighter literary work of a reviewer and editor. In return there finally came to him a reputation greater than that which, in his lifetime, any other English writer had enjoyed.

Fortunate in those days he must have appeared to be, set far above the reach of fate; and the stranger who any morning happened to see him, as he strolled about his estate giving orders for new planting or pruning of trees, must have thought that here at least he had warrant for neglecting the advice of Solon to call no man happy till after his death. But the wisdom of that old and cautious pronouncement was to have a new exemplification when in the January of 1826, the failure of Constable brought Ballantyne's printing house, in which Scott was a partner, down with a crash. The story of the business transactions which resulted in this catastrophe is long and intricate, nor is it possible in a short space to speak of the matter in detail.[1] Every one will agree with the conclusions at which Mr. Hutton arrives, that Ballantyne, though his want of business sense may have been exaggerated, was not a capable business man, and that Scott was too antiquarian in his tastes, and too impulsively kind in regard to the productions of his friends to be a good publisher. But besides this it has, I think, been shown that his conduct was wanting in prudence. Aware that Ballantyne's business was in itself by no means in a satisfactory condition, he went on spending at his usual generous rate, trusting, as it proved, blindly, that Constable, on whose credit, pledged for him and for which he had pledged himself, both he and Ballantyne ultimately relied, was as "firm as Ben Lomond." So high was his trust in Constable that the failure, when it came, came to him as a stunning shock, though looking back now on the three ends of the string, one can see that there was no other likely outcome to the strange tangle of cross liabilities and constant expenditure in

[1] The reader may consult Mr. Leslie Stephen's article in the 'Cornhill Magazine' for April 1897, where the subject is discussed.

which he was mixed up. Curiosity may ask
how far Scott realized that his own lavish outlay
was putting a strain on his resources to which
it was a risk to subject them. All the evidence
goes to show that he thought himself well within
the mark, and it is true that had Constable been
financially sound, Ballantyne's difficulties would,
with the aid of Scott's Midas touch, have proved
temporary. Still it is impossible not to feel that
it was no part of prudence for him, spending
and borrowing as he did, not to have been
exhaustively informed as to the state of his
affairs, or for him, relying devotedly on Constable's soundness, not to have retrenched to
secure that the business in which he was
primarily concerned was reasonably sound. But
if there is something here which makes Scott
at least partially responsible for his own un-
doing, and not, as he has so often been represented, the mere martyr of unavoidable chance,
it was a responsibility of a kind which could
only have attached to a nature generously rich.
Not merely in the way he met his troubles, but
in the course which led to them one catches the
character of the man. When the blow fell, two
courses were open: to surrender what he pos-

sessed, and start life afresh, or to ask for time,
and discharge the heavy burden piece by piece.
Of these courses he took, as all the world knows,
the manlier one. The objections to the first
were indeed patent. By adopting it his house
and cherished possessions would have gone to
strangers, and his creditors obtained perhaps little
more than half what was due. Everything, for
a man of indomitable energy, was in favour of
the second. The way was difficult, but at the
end there was the recompense of household
gods preserved, and in taking it there was the
consolation, dear to a man of worth, that honour
was satisfied. The consequences of an over-
sanguine habit have never been met in a spirit
of more earnest fortitude. To annul the effects
of the catastrophe Scott worked with added
determination, but even he could not support
the strain. Coming at the close of a career, so
full of fruitful industry, untroubled by calamity,
and beyond expectation fortunate, there is an
irresistible pathos in this dying struggle, the last
effort of noble powers; yet something of the
kind was needed to show the resources of that
even and patient character, and to give to his
life that touch of intimate human interest which

an unhappy world misses in the records of too easily successful days.

Sir Walter Scott, to those who are fond of such distinctions, the chief glory of Scottish literature, and to those who are justly proud of common interests, common blood, and common speech, one of the chief glories of the English tongue, lived a life, which, when we consider the variety and compass of his writings, is of perpetual and perplexing interest to his biographers. It was not that his ambitions were those of other men—reputation, wealth, family, and lands. Shakespeare himself was not exempt from these; the purchaser of New Place loved his position of dignity in his native town. Unless great writers are to be entirely free from thoughts of self, and perhaps no one who ever was, was ever a great writer, it is not easy to see how they can avoid sharing the most dignified of personal ambitions, those of family.

> " To join the choir invisible
> Of those immortal dead who live again,"

is but an impalpable immortality at the best, but to live in the affections of descendants, to be associated for generations with the spot of earth

they inherit, is, in a real sense, to escape the
grave. One wonders how many marriages would
be made were it not for this desire, warm and
comforting in the very notion, to live on in a
perpetual series of selves. The visionary or
envious alone despise or affect to despise it,
and it is not here that Scott's life is perplexing.
It is perplexing because it was the life of a
dramatist pure and simple. Shakespeare, no
one can read his plays and doubt it, was not
only a dramatist: he shared—as to the particulars of his opinions of course we shall never
know anything—the passions, doubts, and difficulties of his characters. Scott, and in his case
there is ample evidence to support the assertion,
was a pure narrator. Has he to tell us that a
man was a sceptic, a Jew, a Mohammedan, or
a pagan; that a person was looked at askance
on account of his religion, or trade, or politics;
that a man was enthusiastic in some cause or
interest—he tells us so and is done with it. He
is not warmed or troubled by the hundreds of
differing opinions which find dramatic expression in his pages. One sees here perhaps the
"thread of the attorney," a touch of the legal
method not friendly to deep sympathies, the

working out of the habit too readily learnt in
the law courts, of treating the passions and views
of men as mere material for observation. But
this tendency, though fostered by his training,
was natural to him, and whatever profession he
had followed, would have shown itself. It was
not merely that he had no bias towards enthusiasm—one would not have wished him to have
that—but that he carried his aversion to it so ·
far as often to cramp his interests. He judged
calmly of practice, but at the same time, a price
he need not have paid, he allowed his mind on
its theoretical side to grow cold. Thus, for
instance, where Mr. Hutton says, "Of enthusiasm
in religion Scott always spoke very severely," and
quotes him as complaining to Lord Montague
of such enthusiasm "as makes religion a motive
and a pretext for particular lines of thinking in
politics and temporal affairs," one may be
pardoned if one sees there the practical man.
To appreciate the danger that the actual
business of life should be directed by visionary
dogmas, or that the standard of conduct should
not be that agreeable to the general reason,
but that shifting one seen by differing faiths,
is surely to do no more than to keep one's

grasp on affairs. So to think is no proof that
the speculative side of the mind has withered,
so to think is not to be separated from the
greatest abstract thinkers; but what separated
Scott not only from the greatest thinkers, but
from thinkers of real weight was that he did
not stop here. His distrust of the vagaries
of speculation was a sign of mental health; it
was a serious weakness that with speculation
for its own sake he should have taken no active
concern. Susceptible to moral and religious
impressions in a certain sense he peculiarly was,
but he possessed by nature, and acquired by
training and habit, a dislike to exercising his
mind freely among differences, and, as a consequence, when he came to speak of them he
was not stirred. It was a natural result. He
allowed himself partly consciously, partly un-
consciously, to fall into a groove. He accepted
pleasantly, and if we did not know it from his
life, his novels would be proof enough, the
strange atmosphere about him. A man of great
humanity, he seems never to have seen the
criminal's case against society, nor to have
realized, for example, that duelling, a mode of
settling a dispute which gave fearful odds against

the weak, was a practice he should not sanction. He had no anxiety for discussion, it was natural that people should accept whatever was held in their locality, and unnatural they should not. He was an omnivorous reader, and yet it is difficult to conceive of him as startled out of his customary phlegm by any treatise on government: had he lived to read Schopenhauer's grave and airy discussion on the respective advantages of monogamy and polygamy he would have gone in laughing to dinner, wondering how any one could concern himself with matters so removed from English practice. The religious and moral ideas of his nation came home to him to all appearance easily: a country gentleman, he was content to work along with the views of country gentlemen however some might miss his intellectual approval. It is true it is impossible to tell what passed in the interior of a mind of the calibre of Scott's, but if he experienced that "warfare of the soul" which disturbed Shakespeare's equanimity, it left no trace. Such opinions as he held, he came to hold without the reserve of dubiety, and though always, as a matter of feeling, with good-tempered tolerance, yet with what came near a refusal to reason.   He had heard, but he was not interested in the opposite side; the accident of his surroundings took the edge from his inquiry.

It is simple to say that here, not in his views but in his manner of holding them, in his regarding orthodoxy and commonplace as if they were really matter of course, lies his weakness as a writer, to emphasize the truism that in no such way can a man attain that elasticity of mind which is the general characteristic of the great. It was a damaging attitude doubtless: "Foolish is the wayfaring man," as the old English writer has it, "who takes the smooth way which misleads him, and forsakes the rough one which leads him to the city."   The difficult thing is to explain how it came about that a writer so constituted accomplished the work he did.   One may suppose perhaps that the sympathy of the heart where it exists in sufficient strength will enable an author to dispense at least partially with the sympathy of the head.   Anyhow there must be some explanation how it happens that Scott, the least intellectually sympathetic of great writers, has left a body of work of different and inferior quality indeed, but comparable in amplitude and variety, with the productions of a mind of the width of Shakespeare's. Carlyle said no more than what was true when he said of Scott that it was "of other stuff that great men are made." It is commonly of other stuff, but the enigmatical thing is that it happened otherwise than commonly with one of the greatest of men.

It is the excess of pedantic nicety to deny that epithet to the man, which we grant so readily to his work. A writer is to be judged by his achievement. After all perhaps the distinction between Scott's character and production is one of which it is easy to make too much. In his life there was observable the same play of wide and sympathetic feeling, the same power of humorous and truthful observation, and the same spirit of placid rectitude, while to consider his writings attentively is to find a partial explanation why he who, to say no more, left various fields of mental activity untravelled, has become so especially the companion of men of the most various temperaments. That the Waverley Novels were written by one man, is a statement both the bearing and weight of which we are liable to forget. If we appreciate its significance we shall not only understand the secret of Scott's outstanding greatness, we shall

also gain some idea, since it is on the bulk of
his production that he depends, how it was
possible for him to dispense with qualities we
are accustomed to look for, and to maintain a
consistent sobriety of feeling we are accustomed
to miss in one whose fortune it is to capture the
world by the vital force of a single masterpiece.

And if this was his pre-eminent achievement,
it is necessary to lay stress on it, since its
importance is readily under-estimated by those
to whom the fact has long been familiar.
The earth goes round the sun, we tell a child,
and the child has nothing like the difficulty of
the contemporaries of Galileo in believing it.
Before we realize the improbability of one man's
producing the Waverley Novels, we are told
that they are the production of one author, and
yet on the face of it the statement is so improbable that during the long period of Scott's
carefully guarded anonymity the public as a
whole believed that several hands were engaged
on the marvellous series. Before we can have
any adequate conception of the greatness of his
achievement, we must try to create for ourselves
the same difficulty of belief.

Shakespeare, like every great and various

author, owes his place in part to his variety as well as to his greatness, but Shakespeare owes it only in part. Had he written only one or two of half-a-dozen plays, for example, 'Twelfth Night,' 'Antony and Cleopatra,' 'Hamlet,' 'Othello,' 'Lear,' or 'Macbeth,' his supremacy would still be undisputed. Outside Shakespeare's works there are in our language no fanciful and romantic comedies which can be compared with 'Twelfth Night,' no Roman plays with 'Antony and Cleopatra,' no dramas of thought with 'Hamlet,' no dramas of passion with 'Othello,' and no tragedies as awful as 'Lear' or 'Macbeth.' It was a wonderful thing that the same man who wrote those plays should also have written 'Romeo and Juliet,' 'Henry IV.,' 'Timon of Athens,' and the 'Winter's Tale'; it was a wonderful thing that he should have written more than twenty others. The range, the variety, the exhaustlessness of Shakespeare's mind will always be a familiar topic for wonder, so much so indeed that we are apt to forget how astonishing it was that he should have produced any one of his greater efforts. But Shakespeare, though he owes much to his variety, does not depend

upon it. Of the author of the Waverley Novels
the reverse may be said. His position of pre-
eminence among English novelists is secured
to him from the fact, that he was not only a
great but a prolific and various writer, that he
produced the whole series of admirable works
which stretches from 'Waverley' to 'The Fair
Maid of Perth.'

As to which, in a general sense—and those
who hold views on this subject must be understood to hold them in a general sense—is the
best of these productions, opinion has long been
divided. For the purpose of definitely raising
the question both of their combined and particular merits, it will be convenient to select
several of those for which this high claim has
been advanced. To select all, and so to ensure
the satisfaction of every taste, would be to provide
a list of inordinate length. In the selection of
'Waverley,' 'The Antiquary,' 'Old Mortality,'
'Rob Roy,' 'The Bride of Lammermoor,' and
'St. Ronan's Well,' a *via media* will be found.
Taking these novels, then, it will be our business
not to press any merely individual opinion about
them, but to ask ourselves what rank in public
estimation Scott as a novelist would have held

had he left a few or only one of those books all claiming, according to various criticisms, the honour of being his masterpiece.

'Waverley' and 'Rob Roy' are novels dealing with the period which is covered by the history of the Stuarts. Thackeray has left a novel dealing with the same period, 'The History of Henry Esmond,' and the world if it were given its choice between 'Esmond' and 'Waverley' would not hesitate for long; nay, it is even questionable whether 'Waverley' and 'Rob Roy' together have given more pleasure than Thackeray's book. It was only the other year that Mr. Stevenson, an exquisite essayist and a writer of great power, but not, it will be granted, a novelist to be named with Scott, produced his charming story 'Catriona,' dealing like 'Rob Roy' with Highland character, and though with less, yet with comparable success.

In 'The Antiquary,' as in 'Guy Mannering,' Scott concerned himself chiefly with the portrayal of character, depending there very little upon the effect of his incident, and seeking there no aid from history. Nor does 'The Heart of Midlothian' depend for its effect on its historical detail, on the long excursus on the Porteous

riots, or even on the admirable figures of the
Duke of Argyll and the Queen, and though the
main incident is essential to the story, the novel
stands not so much for the interest of the
narrative as for that its wonderful group of
characters excites. Considering the three as
novels of character, it may be asked if their
characters are more interesting or more life-like
than those drawn by Fielding or Thackeray,
or even on occasion by Smollett, or, to put the
question in a less general form, are Bertram or
Lovel comparable with Pendennis or Tom
Jones: is Lucy Bertram, the most living of the
ladies in the three novels, comparable with
Sophia: are Oldbuck and Edie Ochiltree better
than Colonel Newcome, Parson Adams and
Partridge: are Madge Wildfire, Meg Merrilees
and Jeanie Deans, admirable as they are, beyond
comparison, as pieces of character painting, with
Mrs. Honour, Tabitha Bramble, Becky Sharpe
and Blanche Amory? It will hardly happen
that the answers to all these questions are in
the affirmative: it will be conceded that Scott
here, where as some think he is at his best, does
no more than divide the honours with Fielding
and Thackeray. And if we take the novels as

a whole, the result is not more consistent with the theory of his supremacy. Neither the 'Antiquary,' strong as it is in character, nor 'The Heart of Midlothian,' which has strength both of character and incident, can be placed quite by the side of 'Tom Jones'; and though 'Guy Mannering' is a far less partial picture of life than 'Vanity Fair,' and has none of the rambling prolixity of narrative which disfigures 'Pendennis' and the 'Newcomes,' it is doubtful indeed if it is as brilliant as 'Vanity·Fair,' or as great an achievement as either of Thackeray's two later novels. The 'Antiquary' is a finer work than 'Humphry Clinker,' in every sense a nobler production, but had Scott left only the 'Antiquary,' it would be rash to predict that it would survive Smollett's masterpiece.

'St. Ronan's Well' challenges comparison with the work of two separate schools, with novelists such as Miss Austen, and (while totally different in manner, employing as they do dark colours) with novelists such as Richardson, in so far as it is a novel of domestic character with the one, and in so far as it is a novel of incident with the other, but it is only on the side of its incident that a serious comparison can be made.

" When it came," says Mr. Hutton, " to describing the small differences of manner, differences
not due to external habits, so much as to internal
sentiment or education, or mere domestic circumstance, Scott was beyond his proper field.
In the sketch of St. Ronan's Spa, and the
company at the *table d'hôte*, he is of course
somewhat near the mark,—he was too able a
man to fall far short of success in anything he
really gave to the world ; but it is not interesting. Miss Austen would have made Lady
Penelope Penfeather a hundred times as amusing." In so far then as the novel is one of
domestic character and incident, and though
the Scandal Club, with its rough jests and sombre
merriment, is an effective background for the
main tragedy, 'St. Ronan's Well' does not
distance Miss Austen in her own field, does
not even, in the reliable judgment of Mr. Hutton,
equal her. But 'St. Ronan's Well' is to be
considered as a tragedy, a tragedy that stands
out abruptly from its intentionally frivolous
setting, and for this purpose should be taken
together with 'The Bride of Lammermoor,' a
tragedy of a deeper cast, a poetical tragedy,
while 'St. Ronan's Well' is a tragedy in prose,

but containing no single scene in its different
way more effective than the main situation in
the later novel, where Clara confesses to her
brother, and Mowbray, left alone to consider
the total wreck of his hopes, is startled from his
reverie by the rumbling wheels of Touchwood's
chaise.   It is to be asked if 'St. Ronan's Well,'
with its tragedy breaking in on gay life, is a
greater production than that work of Richardson's, where he also uses a frivolous and humdrum society as a background on which to paint
the sorrows of Clarissa, as it is also to be asked
if 'The Bride of Lammermoor' is an indefinitely greater poetical success than 'The Scarlet
Letter,' 'The Blithedale Romance,' or 'The
Marble Faun'; if Lucy Ashton, the most delicate
of Scott's female portraits, is more alive and
lives more in our thoughts than Hester or
Zenobia or Miriam.   To these questions, which
suggest themselves readily, even prejudice cannot return an equivocal reply.

Of the novels mentioned, 'Old Mortality' is
the last, and with it, at length, our comparisons
are exhausted.   Like 'Rob Roy' and 'Waverley,'
it is a novel dealing with a historical period
and historical events, depending no doubt more

than either of them upon the history introduced, but like them suggesting comparison with Thackeray's 'Esmond.' It does not matter so much that 'Esmond' may stand even this test, that Henry Esmond holds his own with Henry Morton, that the young prince is as good in his way as Claverhouse in his, and that Beatrix towers above Edith Bellenden : the important thing is that here is another novel which challenges comparison, and, as some think, challenges comparison more seriously than either 'Waverley' or 'Rob Roy' with the same great book to which in speaking of them reference was directed. To compare only a few of Scott's fictions with those of other writers is to get a hint of the ground on which his real claim to pre-eminence may be based. It does not consist in the merits of single books. The novels selected belong to three departments, that of the novel cast in a historical period, that of the novel of character, and that of the tragic tale, departments in which all Scott's masterpieces are contained. In none of them does he outrun competition, or if in one of them he does, he does it with difficulty—if 'The Bride of Lammermoor' is better than anything Hawthorne produced, it is not indefinitely better.

In one department alone, and curiously enough in a department in which there is none of those works commonly selected as his masterpieces, he has no rivals. It was a field which before him only indifferent novelists had entered.   In a sense he discovered it. 'Waverley,' 'Rob Roy,' and 'Old Mortality' would be classified by many as historical novels, and so, no doubt, they are if we grant the name to any novel in which historical characters or events are introduced. But their object is not a historical object, and it is more correct to call them novels of character and incident placed in a historical setting.   Such a novel, for instance, is 'Esmond,' and it is only by so describing it, that we shall be able to distinguish it from a novel with so different a purpose as 'Kenilworth.'   There can be no absolute distinction.   The main interest of 'Esmond' is not historical, and the same is true of 'Rob Roy,' but 'Waverley' depends in great measure on the figure and surroundings of Charles Edward, and the chief personage in 'Old Mortality,' Balfour of Burley, is not only historical, but acts, as far as his main actions are concerned, in accordance with history. Nevertheless Scott has a series of novels which can be broadly distinguished from 'Waverley' and 'Old Mortality,' and which produce the same kind of effect that history produces. In such a tale as 'Quentin Durward' we forget the story, and remember only the picture that is there presented of Louis XI and his court. It is of course not always easy to say on which side of a line of this kind any particular novel is to be placed, but what a number of novels has Scott in which the fictitious story that is woven into the historical events, is but a kind of background to them, but threads to bring them together. In 'Kenilworth,' though the history is extremely fictitious, there is quite a small element of intentional fiction.

In those pieces of animated history, in those reigns revivified, what must surprise the reader most is the number of widely differing historical personalities with which Scott has dealt. In 'Ivanhoe' and 'The Talisman' he brings back Richard and his Crusaders, in 'Kenilworth' Elizabeth, in 'The Abbot' Mary Queen of Scots, in 'The Fortunes of Nigel' James I, and in 'Quentin Durward' Louis XI. It would be difficult to select from the whole of history three monarchs more different in character and

habits than Richard and Louis and James, and
though the contrast between Mary and Elizabeth
comes, so to speak, to the hand of every
historical student, it is nowhere more effective
than in Scott's pages.   And this effect he produces, not by the aid of historical learning and
accuracy, for which he was not specially distinguished, but by a species of historical instinct.
For anything like these novels we have to go
back to Shakespeare.   Scott's Elizabeth, his Mary,
his Richard, his Louis, his James, actually live,—
live as vividly in our own imaginations as Shakespeare's Henrys.   His princes are princes as
unmistakably as his peasants are peasants, and
what is more, he can distinguish between them;
he can give the man, not necessarily the exact
historical figure, which is quite another matter,
but the individual and his traits as easily in
their case as when he is dealing with Caleb
Balderstone or Edie Ochiltree.   In one respect
he even surpasses Shakespeare, surpasses him
no doubt because Shakespeare made no effort
in that direction; still he surpasses him in the
truth of his historical atmosphere.   He gets hold
of a historical period in a way Shakespeare
never did.   In 'Ivanhoe' and in 'Kenilworth'

we are in different worlds, whereas it would
puzzle any one who read 'King John' and
'Henry V,' to tell whether the one monarch
did or did not immediately succeed the other.

In this department, Scott among novelists is
supreme, and from the work he achieved here,
from a perusal of 'Quentin Durward' or 'Ivanhoe,' we would be justified in concluding that
he was the first of historical novelists. But to
say so would be to say far too little, he is the
first of English novelists ; and again the question suggests itself—in what is it that his pre-
eminence among English novelists may be said
to consist? It can hardly be on account of his
supremacy in the historical novel pure and
simple, since the historical novel pure and
simple is, by common consent, on a lower plane
of imaginative work than the novel of character
or the novel of serious incident, just as the
historical drama is on a lower plane than the
drama proper. These historical excursions are
of inferior merit, judged as mere achievements,
because the artist is helped by his material, and
judged as productions they are almost necessarily
of inferior merit, because he is almost necessarily
hampered by it. Shakespeare's genius in his

English historical plays is restrained, of course
only in the historical parts, by his desire to be
faithful to the facts; it is not so much restrained
in his Roman plays, because there he had not,
speaking generally, the same historical knowledge, and often not the same historical desire,
and it is not restrained at all in such plays as
'Lear' and 'Macbeth,' because there his desires
were not the desires of a historian. On this
account, and it is theoretical, Scott's accepted
position can hardly be explained by his success
as a historical novelist; if we take the actual
works themselves the matter is still clearer. To
read 'Kenilworth' and 'The Fortunes of Nigel,'
and to consider them as works of the imagination, is to recognize at once that they cannot be
placed above the best works of other English
novelists. Such work is, at least, comparable
with Scott's masterpieces, and there is no reason
why it should fear a comparison with those
novels of his which, though the best in their
particular field, are yet not, considered as
works of imagination, the best things he has
done.

Search as we choose through the Waverley
Novels, we shall not find that there is one of

them which has not to run the risk of a doubtful
judgment when compared with the best work
of other novelists. Scott does not enjoy his
pre-eminence over Richardson, Fielding, Thackeray and Hawthorne as the writer of novels
greater than any which have been written by
those authors ; he enjoys it because he has left
a body of work of more enduring value : it is
not in the heights to which his genius reaches,
but in its amplitude, its untiring excellence
that his pre-eminence consists.

Thackeray has left 'Esmond' and 'Barry
Lyndon,' 'Vanity Fair,' the 'Newcomes' and
'Pendennis.' Against 'Esmond' and 'Barry
Lyndon' the admirer of Scott can place a whole
host of novels cast in a historical setting,
against Thackeray's novels of character, half-a-
dozen admirable efforts, and all this without
trenching on his great tragedies or his novels
of history pure and simple. It is the same with
the other great authors of whom I have spoken.
Not Hawthorne with his extraordinary insight
into the intricacies of mental character, nor
Richardson with his fascinating tediousness and
unquestioned tragic power, nor Fielding with
his abundant and generous life can swing back

the doors of any such extended gallery, or throw
open to us so large a world.   The amplitude of
Scott's genius is not more remarkable than its
unvarying excellence.   In the novel of character
Fielding alone can produce a composition which
need not fear comparison with Scott's best ; in
the novel cast in a historical period he is eclipsed,
if indeed when we think of 'Old Mortality' he
is eclipsed, only by one book of Thackeray's ; in
the prose tragedy with a poetical excellence it
is Hawthorne alone who comes beside him ; 'St.
Ronan's Well' is a worthy successor to Richardson's infinitely greater book, while in the historical novel Scott has beaten the ablest of his
successors and imitators.   He is always to be
compared with the best ; he could do as well as
anybody, or almost as well as anybody, whatever
he attempted, and he has attempted and achieved
far more than any other English novelist has
either achieved or attempted.

   This is the claim, it seems to me, which is to be
made for him as a novelist, and it is this which
justifies criticism, though it is not able to point
to any individual novels of his which take an
undisputed place, in assigning to his work as a
whole a place of undisputed supremacy.   Richard-

son and Hawthorne with all their excellences
have limited fields, Smollett has a field exceedingly limited, even Fielding's range is circumscribed, while Thackeray's is nothing like so wide
as Scott's. All these great authors moreover
have a manner of looking at life : Richardson
approaches it circumspectly and with an eye to
the shadows, Hawthorne with the intention of
lingering delicately, Smollett in rough good
humour, Fielding bravely careless, and Thackeray
with a smile alternately caustic and tender. But
Scott has no manner ; he opens his eyes and
jots down quietly everything he sees. "The
second and third volumes of a strange book
entitled ' Tales of my Landlord,'" said Mrs. Piozzi,
referring to 'Old Mortality,' "are very fine in
their way. People say, ''Tis like reading Shakespeare.' I say, 'Tis as like Shakespeare as a bottle
of peppermint-water is to a bottle of the finest
French brandy." At this distance of time we
see the merit of both judgments. Though it is
quite true that Scott does not see a tenth part
of what Shakespeare saw, he has the same impersonal manner of recording what he sees, and
thus it happened that it was possible to suppose
that the author of 'Old Mortality' was not the

author of 'Ivanhoe,' nor the author of 'The Bride of Lammermoor.'

And if he has the impersonal manner of Shakespeare, he has another affinity to him in the breadth of his range. Like Shakespeare, he found both comedy and tragedy equally natural, and roamed at will wherever his fancy led. Like Shakespeare he presents us with a world of almost infinite variety ; in the works of both we find ourselves in the streets of some great capital, among all conditions of men, and where every interest is found. The variety of his characters indeed is justly comparable with Shakespeare's, in his pages almost every profession and almost every class has its representatives.

But the comparison with Shakespeare goes no further : to see that one needs only to remember Scott's general habit of mind. "The soul's dark cottage," says Waller, in lines that keep alive a once famous name—

" The soul's dark cottage, battered and decayed,
Lets in new light through chinks which time has made"—

but the troubles that fell to Scott were matter of fact, and met in a matter-of-fact manner.

At the end of his life as at the beginning he
found life solid and satisfying, and consequently
though he touches Shakespeare on one side he
is still far away.   He had all of his characteristics
that were possible for a man whatever his breadth
of view, however impersonal his standpoint, however generously sympathetic by temperament,
who had not the faculties, and who had not
undergone the discipline of the great poets.
Of Shakespeare's profound thought he had
nothing; to Shakespeare's deep and concentrated feeling he was almost a stranger.   It is
evident in his poetry, where, far more than in
the novel, the poetical faculties are in request.
Never was there a more happy inspiration than
that which induced him to turn from verse : a
poet of fine feeling, and, at his best, of an admirable plainness, his real work was in prose.
The limitations that told against him as a poet
did not tell against him in anything like the same
degree as a writer of novels, and it is curious
to notice how in his new vehicle of expression,
so well adapted to his genius, he even in some
measure overcame them.   But for the accident
of form, there is more genuine poetry in 'The
Bride of Lammermoor' than in the whole of

'Marmion.' However, even in his novels the limitations remained : he did not feel, except on the rarest occasions,[1] as the great poets feel, with that surprising directness of sympathy which lays bare to us our unknown selves ; he never wandered, as the great poets wander, among those thoughts perplexed which lie at the back of every brain. For this reason, the difference between Scott's success, wonderful as it was, and Shakespeare's success is a difference in kind. As Carlyle truly says, "the difference between Scott and Shakespeare is literally immense : they are of a different species ; the value of the one is not to be counted in the coin of the other," and he goes on, "we might say in a short word which covers a long matter that your Shakespeare fashions his characters from the heart outwards : your Scott fashions from

---

[1] One is that instanced by Mr. Trollope in his life of Thackeray, the death of Bothwell in 'Old Mortality.'

"Die, wretch !—die !" said Balfour, redoubling the thrust with better aim ; and, setting his foot on Bothwell's body as he fell, he a third time transfixed him with his sword.—"Die, bloodthirsty dog ! die as thou hast lived ! —die, like the beasts that perish—hoping nothing—believing nothing."

" And fearing nothing !" said Bothwell. But the passage suffers when divorced from its context.

the skin inwards, never getting near the heart
of them." Of all the sentences brimful of provo-
cation which Carlyle wrote, there is perhaps not
one which has provoked more adverse literary
criticism than this last, and yet, when allowance
is made for the writer's effective habit of speech,
there is no doubt that some such distinction
exists. The tag of the sentence, that Scott never
got near the heart of his characters, may be left
to share the fate of tags, but with this exception
all that Carlyle here says is what it requires no
excess of critical sanity to accept as true : Shakespeare knows his characters far more intimately
than Scott. Scott—who can doubt it?—saw in
the personages he has chosen to represent, in
Saunders Mucklebackit, in Claverhouse, in
Lucy Ashton, infinitely more than the most
acute of mere observers could have seen : he
knew their feelings, their thoughts, and their
fancies, or all of them with which they were
themselves familiar : he knew them, it might be
said, as well as they knew themselves. He could
penetrate beneath the skin, not it is true of an
exceedingly intricate character,[1] but of almost all

[1] Rashleigh, intended as an intricate character study, is
a failure. Perceiving this, his creator wearied of the task,

his characters, and represent them not merely as
they appeared to the world, or as they appeared
to their friends, but as they seemed to themselves.
Shakespeare however can do more than this.

There is nothing more remarkable to the
reader of the Waverley Novels, when he comes
to think about them, than the rarity of the
occasions on which he has been surprised, startled
back, as it were, into himself. But in Shakespeare, these sudden surprises, these master
touches of the poet are of the commonest occurrence : again and again the reader lays down
the book to wonder if he is in reality the infinitely intricate animal who there stands revealed.
Scott's characters rarely surprise us : in the
main, though there are exceptions, their development is methodically consistent ; but Shakespeare's characters are continually surprising us,
the plan of our ideas is not large enough to hold
them ; when we begin to be satisfied that we
have their measure, that we know the capacities
of their beings and our own, Shakespeare takes

---

and when Rashleigh appears at the end of 'Rob Roy' he
is a common villain enough. Compare Scott's success with
such a character as Rob Roy, where the characteristics
are striking but not contradictory.

his key and unlocks a hidden door. And this
is the office of the great poets : in his degree it
is Wordsworth's office, in a supreme degree it is
Shakespeare's office, to flood with a sudden light
the mind itself. To see the difference between
this manner and Scott's it is necessary only to
indicate a familiar comparison, that between
Ravenswood and Hamlet. In the Master of
Ravenswood Scott sees not merely a melancholy
figure, but a melancholy man, and he gives us
from the stores of his generous genius the picture
of the man himself, his actions, his habits, his
waking thoughts. Shakespeare, on the other
hand, sees in Hamlet a mind diseased ; he thinks
with him, for a time he is Hamlet ; nay, he is
more, there is not a half formed fancy, not a
movement of Hamlet's brain with which he is
not familiar. Were the Master of Ravenswood
to spring to life, he would be struck with wonder
at Scott's insight, he would cry out in astonishment that any one should know so much of him,
but if Hamlet were vivified he would not immediately recognize himself, and he would ask,
as it has come to every one to ask, somewhere
or sometime, in reading Shakespeare's plays—Is
this I ?

Work of this kind is not to be found in the Waverley Novels. To their author the world in its perplexity did not lie open, and what attracted him was rather the variety than the difficulty of life. But how wide a field was that over which he swept his kindly eyes!—so wide indeed that there is no absurdity in viewing his achievement by the light of the greatest achievement in literature. Something of what Shakespeare accomplished in poetry, Scott accomplished in prose.

CHAPTER II

THERE has long been a controversy, an impossible controversy, between certain men of affairs and certain literary men, as to the responsibility of fictitious literature for general depravity, and more especially for juvenile depravity. The controversy is impossible since those on one side look at literature from a mistaken though natural standpoint, the standpoint of practical morality, and those on the other take up the indefensible position that literature has no effect upon the character.

The object of art being to tell the truth, not necessarily only apparent truth, which is the province of that branch of art nicknamed realism, but the essential truth about man and his surroundings, the nearer a poet comes to doing this, the nearer a dramatist or a novelist comes to doing it, the nearer he is to artistic

G

success. Actions undertaken for the general welfare, and actions performed to serve some private end must find a place in the pages of a good artist as readily as exiled Dukes and Macbeths, Desdemonas and Cleopatras.

If an imaginative writer chooses to paint the world either as wholly vicious, or wholly virtuous, he is making just the same kind of mistake as if he were to leave out women or omit all notice of men. To give instances that are not disputable : if he chooses to represent vice as invariably successful, and always productive of enduring happiness, he is giving a wrong impression of the supremacy in the world of interests that are selfish ; if he chooses to represent virtue as always materially rewarded, he is giving a wrong impression of the supremacy in the world of interests making for the benefit of others; in both cases he is departing from the truth which is his immediate and only concern. In both cases also he is giving an artificial stimulus, a stimulus greater than that of actual life, to the courses which he happens to represent as attended by such unusually fortunate results; but this is not his real fault, any more than it is the real fault of a winding stream, that it

takes along with it in its windings any wood
that happens to fall in.   The object of an artist ___
being truth, he is to be judged by his adherence
to it or his deviation from it, and not by, what
is to him a purely subsidiary matter, the effects
produced, and though, as the magistrates distinguishing would say, in one of the highly
fanciful cases given, the author is giving an artificial stimulus to immorality and in the other to
morality, there is no real artistic difference
between the two offences—except perhaps that
to represent the world as immaculate is even
more of a caricature than to represent it as
wholly depraved.   An author has no more business to distort the facts in favour of what is
received as moral than he has to distort them in
favour of what is received as immoral, and to
represent that he has is to do incalculable mis-
chief.   This would be the true answer to return .
to the magistrates, not that imaginative literature has no effect upon the character, a point
which they are better qualified to decide than
literary men, but that imaginative literature
has higher interests to consider than those of
effect, the interests of truth, and that, since it is
manifestly impossible for the functionaries of

any state to decide on so complicated a question as the real proportion in the world of selfish and unselfish interests, any interference of theirs could only result in the increase of one kind of lying at the expense of another. It would be the true answer, even if it were true that it was the habit of artists to occupy themselves with the world at large, and not, as is infinitely more usual, only with the piece of it to which they direct their gaze, or which they are able to see.

It would be a harsh demand to make of imaginative writers, and as a matter of literary excellence it would be utopian to expect, that their works, when considered as a whole, should give a fair picture of the whole world, but to lay it down that each separate work of theirs should do so would be out of reason fanciful. Smollett in 'Humphry Clinker' does not deal with the whole world, he makes no pretence of doing so. He does not touch on the world that is open to the poet and the philosopher; he deals with that part of it alone, and it is a large one, which is open to the average man, the man with five senses. Webster's world in 'The Duchess of Malfi' is, it has been said with admirable truth, "a world of horrid crimes and fatal dispositions,"

and that in which we live is something more than
this.   Even Shakespeare, wide as is his range,
does not attempt to crowd the whole field of
observation into a single play.   He shifts his
gaze from point to point, giving to one drama a
tone of meditation, steeping another in the
shadow of disaster, introducing us here to a
world of passion, and there to a world of crime.
No doubt in the long run, and on people who
are competent to understand them, Shakespeare's
plays produce a moral effect.   They produce it
much in the same way—not entirely in the same
way, for we have the ordering insight of the poet
to help us—as a large and varied experience
produces it.   But I suppose an entirely foolish
person might find no experience large or varied
enough to teach him wisdom, and get some
harm even from Shakespeare as a whole.   He is
even more likely to get harm if he reads only a
few of Shakespeare's plays, or the works of other
authors, who, knowing the scope of their genius,
do not pretend to universality.   What is to prevent a man without sufficient ballast, from being
flung after reading Lear into a condition of
nerveless despondence, from learning from
Othello only that the world is an unresisting

prey to the animal passions, or from concluding
when he peruses Fielding's masterpiece, or
Richardson's, that he would find his essential
happiness in modelling his character on that of
either of the heroes of these books? It is no im-
peachment of Shakespeare; great literature was
not written for entirely foolish people, any more
than the world was made for them, and they are
as likely to suffer when they come to deal with
the one as when they come to deal with the
other. Every day and every generation there
are those who find the world a good teacher, as
there are those who complain that she is a hard
mistress who teaches evil. The world would
not be our world if we could not extract from it
gall as well as honey; great authors would not
be great authors if they did not speak truly of
the world. If an author speaks truly, if he
represents his selfish characters as occasionally
possessing attraction, if he represents his unselfish characters as occasionally repellent, if he
allows the good often to meet defeat, and the
bad often to attain success, it must be as possible to extract harm from his pages as it is
possible to extract harm from the world.

To say of an imaginative writer, as is so

frequently and proudly said of Scott, that it is impossible to extract from his volumes anything that is harmful, is in reality to say that he did not speak the whole truth about man or society; it is to lay emphasis on his capital defect. It is not so much, as French criticism urges, that he was over-nice, sensitive to the proprieties beyond what the tone of his age required, for this over-niceness of his, though seriously limiting the range of his activity, did not often affect[1] his treatment of those subjects which he did select. It is rather that he was constantly the prey—those who remember 'The Bride of Lammermoor' will allow that he was not always the prey—of a desire to see virtue rewarded. Things do not fall out in the world altogether so sweetly as they fall out in his novels. Lost heirs are not so often found, death-bed repentances are not so common, strong villains, when they run atilt against wounded heroes, are not so subject to apoplectic fits, sisters who prefer a rigid altruism to their instincts have sometimes to pay the price of their

[1] A forcible instance to the contrary is to be found in 'St. Ronan's Well,' where Scott, with an unpleasing deference to public opinion, as foreshadowed by his publisher, minimized the circumstances which led up to the catastrophe, and with which alone it was reasonable.

austerity, and all the bad women are not dead. The history of mankind, so confused and darkened, is not a fairy tale, and if Scott has more than once made it appear so, he is the lesser artist on that account.

This is a limitation which attaches to the Waverley Novels as a whole. Their author, both as a writer and a moralist, is too facile and pleasing to convince. But though disposing of events as he does, he misses the reward which the cold and thankless service of Donna Vera in her good time brings, work so varied and so magnificent cannot but be fruitful of profit. In becoming the idol of surface moralists, he has paid the full penalty for his defects. Moral excellence, and of the same kind as Shakespeare's, Scott has in his degree, not on account but in despite of his elegant falsehoods; he owes it to his artistic excellence, which, when all deductions are allowed, is so great, to the width and essential truth of the world which he opens to us, and from contact with which we may learn far more simply than in actual life, many of the main truths which experience will teach.

The central incidents of his story he is too apt to twist into conformity with a cut and dried

scheme of rewarding and punishing, with the —
result that while satisfying his fancy, the picture
he presents is both too brightly and too darkly —
coloured. To consider his novels as a whole, is
to have the criticism suggested, that wherever it
is the character that attracts his attention he is
most excellent, even the action is most excellent ;
but that when he busies himself with action for
its own sake, great as is his occasional success,
he frequently loses his hold on things. When
he lets events happen he is strong, when he
proceeds to spin a story he is often weak. In
the hands of a great master the method most
successfully adopted seems always the most
natural, but it is proper to remember that
Shakespeare is never stronger than when he is
doing just that, in doing which Scott is seldom
at his best. Shakespeare at his best has no idea
of letting a story tell itself anyhow, of allowing
it to shift along to suit the needs of the slowly
developing characters: like the angel which
brought fortune to Addison, he "rides in the
whirlwind, and directs the storm." The only
novel in which Scott has adopted this manner
of Shakespeare's with consistent success is
'The Bride of Lammermoor.' In general, and

largely because he was a great novelist and not a
great dramatist, his manner where successful was
different; his interest was in character, and when
his gaze was concentrated on his characters he
rarely made a mistake.　Not that a novelist can
afford to despise action; to do so is to become a
Miss Austen and not a Scott; but that the genius
of the novel inclining in another direction, he is
likely to err when he devotes exclusive attention
to it.

From this point of view, 'The Antiquary' is
the novel which is fullest of instruction for the
critic.　The main interest is centred in a group of
characters depicted with loving accuracy.　The
world in which Oldbuck, the Mucklebackits, and
Edie Ochiltree move is the real world; in the
whole of the Waverley Novels there is no healthier
or saner atmosphere, but the backbone of the
story, that part of it on which the fortunes of the
hero turn, has no real relation with the characters
displayed: it is out of tone, foisted in like a
fragment from 'Macbeth' among the greenwood
of 'As You Like It.'　This story, intended partly
to sustain the reader's interest by a series of
striking events, and partly to show the operation
of certain moral laws, working, it may be said, by

no means so much without exception as artists turned moralists suppose, fails as a morality because it is unreal, and as a record of action because it is superfluous. However, no one remembers it, no one cares in the least about the Earl of Glenallan or his bad and dead mother, or the desperate occurrences with which they are connected. With our pleasure while we are reading the novel they may interfere, but they do not intrude themselves upon our recollection.

'The Antiquary,' first published in 1816, was the third of Scott's novels in order of production. In his Advertisement to the first edition he speaks of the three as follows—

"The present work completes a series of fictitious narratives, intended to illustrate the manners of Scotland at three different periods. 'Waverley' embraced the age of our fathers, 'Guy Mannering' that of our own youth, and 'The Antiquary' refers to the last ten years of the eighteenth century. I have, in the two last narratives especially, sought my principal personages in the class of society who are the last to feel the influence of that general polish which assimilates to each other the manners of different nations."

Something then, as he elsewhere tells us, of the licence of the historical novelist, Scott always assumed to himself. By throwing the scene a little back from his day he was enabled to dispense with the minute accuracy in point of detail expected from a novelist who deals with manners immediately contemporary, and to devote a greater part of his attention to the truth of nature. The device was singularly happy. Speaking of a time just past, he availed himself of the licence of the historical novelist, without, as was essential for novels dealing with character and manners as much as with events, losing familiarity with the customs depicted.

As a novel of character, 'The Antiquary' is the most remarkable of Scott's productions. Nowhere is he a more faithful observer of the turns which differing personalities take, nowhere does he give a more living picture of human beings, and this he does without aid from incident. Given the story of 'Old Mortality,' there are many novelists who could have written not 'Old Mortality' indeed, but a good novel. A bad one, with the story of 'The Antiquary,' almost any novelist but Scott would have written. Properly speaking, there are two stories in 'The Antiquary,' the first extremely simple, the ostensible object of which is only to bring the characters together, and the second long and detailed, containing the bulk of the plot. A young man about whom nothing is known, and probably as in fairy tales a prince in disguise, has a series of uneventful adventures. As far as the story is concerned the interest of the reader is not excited till he perceives that the mystery will somehow be cleared up. All that precedes is merely a preamble to the tale of wrong and injury which is bound up with the fortunes of the house of Glenallan. It is instructive to notice how Scott, in whom the genius of the novel shows itself at every turn, makes use of those two sets of incidents. Out of the simple materials of the first he constructs a perfectly natural story sufficient to allow of the development of a variety of characters. Oldbuck, going his rounds as the laird of Monkbarns, introduces us to the Mucklebackits, a family of fishers, and to Edie Ochiltree, a wandering beggar. Lovel, becoming a guest at Oldbuck's house, introduces us to its inmates, Miss Grizel, Mary M'Intyre, her brother Hector, and the dependents Caxton and Jenny. Sir Arthur Wardour's credulity brings us into contact with the amusing Douster-swivel, the general curiosity in the village about Lovel affords opportunity for the portrayal of a

number of rustic characters, while the rising of
the tide brings out the deeper and more serious
side of the principal personages. It is a matter
of difficulty for an author to give in any single
production the benefits of a large experience.
But in ' The Antiquary,' as in many of his greater
productions, Scott manages to do so. One feels
that the delineator of Oldbuck is familiar with a
world of extensive range. His treatment of the
second set of incidents is equally interesting.
There, no doubt, he is wide of the mark; he
stumbles perfunctorily through his farrago of
adventure, which, if an argument to ' The Antiquary' were to be written, would take up the
greater part, throwing no new light upon his
characters and producing no pleasure, but also
somehow, and this it is that shows how admirable
his instinct was, without leaving anything that
clings to the memory or destroys the effect of
the vital part of the book. Had a lesser artist
written 'The Antiquary,' a novelist with a less
safe instinct for his art, the memory of Lord
Glenallan and his dark ancestors, figures suited
to the kind of tragedy in vogue last century,
would have been all we should have carried
away. To combine the two sets of incidents

without detriment to the one or the other was of course impossible, but that he should even perfunctorily have attempted it throws a curious light upon Scott's manner of working. To find Lovel a family and fortune was no such difficult task, as to preclude its being done soberly, nor was there anything to prevent Scott's telling us, had he been content to shape the second part of the story to what his genius had made of the first, that the mystery was no great mystery after all, and that Lovel had left his home under a cloud of suspicion which like other clouds finally lifted. For the introduction of improbabilities there was no real necessity. If they were to be introduced, if the reader's interest was to be excited by new and surprising occurrences, how easy it would have been for a writer of Scott's resource to have effected his purpose in another manner! A touch of confidence would have propitiated the reader, and even a totally un-looked-for shower of material blessings accom-panied by a suspicion of laughter, a light-hearted journey into the land where the long-lost heirs of great houses play with ingots of silver would have passed as the *dénouement* of a novel. Flights of fancy are not to be eyed too strictly, and if the

poet or novelist ends his tale laughing it must be
a preposterous conclusion that will give offence.
There was never the reader of ' As You Like It '
who was displeased with Duke Frederick's sudden
conversion. The matter is otherwise where no
such concession is made. Serious improbabilities
come oddly in the midst of a plain narrative,
and to introduce in a work-a-day world a sombre
melodrama is what, one would think, no great
author would attempt.

It is generally rash to lay down abstract pro-
positions, but it may at least be said that it is
extremely troublesome to introduce Tragedy in
Comedy. Comedy, as Shakespeare and Scott
have shown, may be employed to give relief to
feelings excited by Tragedy. Tragedy is a strain
upon the feelings, and to introduce a spice of
Comedy, not in itself inconsistent with the tragic
intentions of the artist, and even where the
result is to intensify the gloom, is to shift the
strain. The reader is grateful for the rest.
But a man who reads a comedy does not hope,
does not expect that his feelings will suddenly
be harrowed. The least touch of caprice in a
call upon his emotions will perplex and annoy
him, and consequently if Tragedy is to be in-

troduced in Comedy, and especially if it is to be introduced in a comedy of manners, it must be done by the most gentle of transitions; the tragic incident must have nothing improbable about it, nothing that depends upon the excitation of the imaginative faculty ; it must spring naturally out of the concerns of every day.   That these are commonplaces is true, but it is also true that they are commonplaces which Scott in the main action of ' The Antiquary ' sets at defiance.   It is the more surprising since when he was content to take things as they came, and not to trouble himself with fantastic stories of guilt and retribution, he had perhaps as much as any man, and certainly more than any English novelist, the rare power of slipping from the domain of Comedy into that of passion and feeling, of showing how amid the concerns of ordinary life the heart may be stirred.   Indeed he is nowhere more powerful than here.   It is difficult to introduce Tragedy in Comedy, but he has done it often; his sympathy is so human that he passes with the gentlest of transitions from mere matter of fact to the poetry that so often lies beneath it ; he knew the secret, as Wordsworth knew the secret, of making a little action great.

H

The following scene from ' The Antiquary,' to which it is only necessary to premise that Mucklebackit's eldest son Steenie had been drowned, while fishing, a few days before, will serve better than further comment—

"When Oldbuck came in front of the fisherman's hut, he observed a man working intently, as if to repair a shattered boat which lay upon the beach, and, going up to him, was surprised to find it was Mucklebackit himself. ' I am glad,' he said, in a tone of sympathy—' I am glad, Saunders, that you feel yourself able to make this exertion.'

"' And what would ye have me to do,' answered the fisher gruffly, ' unless I wanted to see four children starve, because ane is drowned? It's weel wi' you gentles, that can sit in the house wi' handkerchers at your een when ye lose a friend ; but the like o' us maun to our wark again, if our hearts were beating as hard as my hammer.'

"Without taking more notice of Oldbuck he proceeded in his labour ; and the Antiquary, to whom the display of human nature under the influence of agitating passions was never indifferent, stood beside him, in silent attention, as if watching the progress of the work. He observed more than once the man's hard features, as if by the force of association, prepare to accompany the sound of the saw and hammer with his usual symphony of a rude tune hummed or whistled, and as often a slight twitch of convulsive expression showed that, ere the sound was uttered, a cause for suppressing it rushed upon his mind. At length, when he had patched a considerable rent, and was beginning to mend another, his feelings appeared altogether to derange the power of attention

necessary for his work. The piece of wood which he
was about to nail on was at first too long ; then he sawed
it off too short ; then chose another equally ill adapted
for the purpose. At length, throwing it down in anger,
after wiping his dim eye with his quivering hand, he
exclaimed, ' There is a curse either on me or on this auld
black bitch of a boat, that I have hauled up high and dry,
and patched and clouted sae mony years, that she might
drown my poor Steenie at the end of them, an' be d—d
to her !' and he flung his hammer against the boat, as if
she had been the intentional cause of his misfortune.
Then recollecting himself, he added, ' Yet what needs ane
be angry at her, that has neither soul nor sense ?—though
I am no that muckle better mysell. She's but a rickle o'
auld rotten deals nailed thegither, and warped wi' the
wind and the sea—and I am a dour carle, battered by
foul weather at sea and land till I am maist as senseless as
hersell. She maun be mended though again' the morning
tide—that's a thing o' necessity.'

"Thus speaking, he went to gather together his in-
struments and attempt to resume his labour, but Oldbuck
took him kindly by the arm. 'Come, come,' he said,
'Saunders, there is no work for you this day—I'll send
down Shavings the carpenter to mend the boat, and he
may put the day's work into my account—and you had
better not come out to-morrow, but stay to comfort your
family under this dispensation, and the gardener will
bring you some vegetables and meal from Monkbarns.'

'I thank ye, Monkbarns,' answered the poor fisher ;
' I am a plain-spoken man, and hae little to say for mysell ;
I might hae learned fairer fashions frae my mither lang
syne, but I never saw muckle gude they did her ; however, I thank ye. Ye were aye kind and neighbourly,
whatever folk says o' your being near and close ; and I hae
often said in thae times when they were ganging to raise

up the puir folk against the gentles—I hae often said, ne'er a man should steer a hair touching to Monkbarns while Steenie and I could wag a finger—and so said Steenie too. And, Monkbarns, when ye laid his head in the grave, (and mony thanks for the respect), ye saw the mouls laid on an honest lad that likit you weel, though he made little phrase about it.'

"Oldbuck, beaten from the pride of his affected cynicism, would not willingly have had any one by upon that occasion to quote to him his favourite maxims of the Stoic philosophy. The large drops fell fast from his own eyes, as he begged the father, who was now melted at recollecting the bravery and generous sentiments of his son, to forbear useless sorrow, and led him by the arm towards his own home."

It is in such passages, into which the narrative imperceptibly glides, that Scott's power of truthful observation is especially revealed. He is not more truthful here than when he is dealing with the crotchets of the Antiquary, or with the manners of Edie Ochiltree, but his truthfulness is more apparent. As in the world we do not know any one till sorrow has touched him, so Scott's characters are so much a part of the world we see, that but for such incidents we should miss their best part. A lesser artist, without that height of self-reliance which is the prerogative of conscious power, would have told us plainly and at length all of which he conceived

Oldbuck's nature to be capable, or, despising this, would have invented some trivial accidents to show early the full variety of the character. A different artist working by a more poetical method would from the beginning, no matter if the circumstances were ordinary, have given us the key to the man. Scott is content to wait till in the course of the narrative everything is shown. As patient as Richardson, though far less tedious, he unrolls a bit· of the world and lets his characters go their way. They appear and impress us, just as they appear and impress Lovel, just as they would appear and impress us in actual life. Lovel meets a chance acquaintance by the ferry, and we see this stranger then as he would be seen by any passer-by, a testy, somewhat crotchety, but withal good-humoured man. He does not open himself to Lovel at once. We are not at once told all, but gradually as he warms to his young companion, the most striking of his crotchets begins to obtrude itself. It is the Antiquary who shows Lovel the Roman remains, it is the Antiquary who quarrels with Sir Arthur, and it is only little by little, when the party of his friends are caught by the tide, when he goes to Lovel with his kindly offer of assistance, when he assures Mucklebackit that he will pay for a day's carpentering, that Old-buck comes before us. Nothing could be more natural than this, for what can be more natural than simple nature? Nothing in its own way could be finer, and nothing, if we exclude those occasions on which a call is made on the highest poetical art, more artistic. The more we read about Scott's characters the better we know them ; the more he writes about them the further he works himself into their heart. It is amazing to see how patiently, his mind being made up that his patience would be rewarded, he sets himself to develop the intricacies of an interest-ing nature. To the thoughtless Edinburgh student, to the self-communing Edinburgh pro-fessor, what was Andrew Gemmels but a pictur-esque, intrusive, and impertinent beggar? What was he more at the first look to a particular Edinburgh student with whom the world has concern? But the excellence of this student was that with him the first look was seldom the last. To see in Andrew Gemmels something more than others saw was indeed but the fruit of a closer and more patient scrutiny, but to see in him Edie Ochiltree was to bring the creative imagination to work on what had been observed. However, Scott does not drift from his moorings; if he sees a statue in a block of marble it is out of that identical piece of marble that the statue is to be hewn. When Ravenswood bids farewell to Lucy, he repeats the words ascribed to him in the old legend on which 'The Bride of Lammermoor' was founded; the circumstances of Jeanie Deans are closely analogous to those of Helen Walker; and Edie at his first entrance with his "Praetorian here and Praetorian there," does not essay a flight—except that the humour of no real beggar was ever so spontaneous an outgrowth—beyond the capacity of his real counterpart. He is a personage, interesting certainly, but chiefly interesting from the strong dash of insolence in his sturdy independence. If this is to mimic to the life, it is still to mimic, but the arts of a however admirable and inartificial mimicry are left behind as Edie comes more prominently forward, as Scott makes him and the reader well acquainted, as we see developing before us the possibility of great strength and resource, and a capacity for extraordinary loyalty. Here again there is no effort of the author, circumstances speak for him; it is not an intrusive beggar whom at the end of the book we see standing silent before the magistrate. But perhaps in the whole of this masterpiece there is no better instance of Scott's power of elucidating character than that afforded by his treatment of the family of Mucklebackit. They are fishers, and what is the business of fishers but to sell fish? We should be astonished to find them doing anything else, and consequently at the beginning of the book we find them doing that, chaffering with Jenny or Miss Grizel, or Oldbuck, and just as if Scott was not to find among them some of the finest even of his pictures of the troubles of the poor, the simple funeral, and the grief of Saunders.

'The Antiquary' affords also a number of admirable instances of Scott's method of dealing with his less complicated characters, if indeed the method is not less a different one than the same method applied to different circumstances. A good-natured servant-wench, a well-behaved girl, a typical Scotch gentlewoman, a hectoring captain, a loquacious barber, a German charlatan, these are characters which need no probing; an ordinary observer is competent to grasp the whole of them at once, and consequently in

each case there is a particularity in their introduction. We are told more about them on
their first appearance, than we are told about
Oldbuck or Edie. In daylight they would be
clear enough, and in the Waverley Novels we
are in daylight. Jenny, Mary M'Intyre, Miss
Grizel, Captain M'Intyre, Caxton and Douster-
swivel—what would we miss in these characters
if we met them in the society of Fairport?
Little; and so Scott spends some time in showing us, by the aid of his humorous touchstone,
just what they are, and in telling us all about
them. Thus with his simpler as with his more
intricate characters his method is in reality the
same. It is as if experience were to take us by
the hand and to explain to us how she works.
The great dramatic poets have another manner.
In their productions we do not merely find experience compressed, we are brought into contact
with an admirable and instantaneous intuition.
We get on terms as quickly with their intricate
as with their simple characters. Hamlet, for
example, springs on the page as Pallas from the
head of Zeus all armed. For all purposes we
know him as well at the end of the first act
as at the end of the fifth; but it is idle to

emphasize the distinction almost essential between a novelist dealing with a world of prose
and a dramatist in his most rapid and poetical
moods. To bring the man before us immediately needs not only the insight of the poet,
but often his constant reliance on striking
and poetical events. In depicting character
generally, and especially in that part of 'The
Antiquary' which deals with mundane affairs,
Scott adopts a method that comes more naturally
to a novelist. For a novel, when all is said, is a
familiar tale, and we catch its peculiar note most
easily where the novelist ambles familiarly along
without troubling himself with the arts of
dramatic construction. The best part of 'The
Antiquary' shows the novel doing work which
the drama has not patience to accomplish, work
too of infinite value, since it is not given to
every one to follow the poets into their sudden
and elemental world. To read the book is
not certainly to have the imagination greatly
quickened, but to read it—to read of Edie, of
Oldbuck and his household—is to see the plain
everyday world as we should not otherwise see
it, till circumstances and trouble had enlarged
and softened our vision. It is a high panegyric

of a man's work to say that it affects us in the same manner as life; it is a still higher one to say that it gives to youth the power of seeing life as it is seen by the experienced and kind.

It is not often that one finds among the Waverley Novels a book like 'The Antiquary,' of which one can confidently affirm that it would be just as good as it is had the goodly art of play-writing never come into existence. In a country like England, in which there was so long established a dramatic tradition, it was impossible that the authors of a new form of imaginative effort should not feel the influence of the old. To the novel the drama left many obvious legacies, among others a belief in the importance of action, in the necessity of dis-criminated characters and striking situations. In the sphere of character, so early as the time of Richardson, the novel had left the drama behind, and though it could not be hoped that in the sphere of action the newer form would maintain its ground, it was clear that even there it would ultimately learn something from the old rival it has now gone so far to displace. What is surprising, since great artists are in general not only familiar with the resources of

their medium, but in the habit of stretching
them to the utmost, is that up to Scott's day
the modern novel should have borrowed so little.
For a long time it went its leisurely course; if
it had a dramatic story, spinning it out, as in
'Clarissa,' with interminable detail; and if it
had not, as in 'Pamela,' 'Humphry Clinker,' or
'Evelina,' allowing the story to go as it pleased,
provided the characters were displayed. With
Scott it was no longer so; in his hands the
novel does everything, now as in 'The Bride of
Lammermoor' joining issue with the drama in
a whole book, now as in 'Old Mortality' abound-
ing in dramatic situations, and now as in 'The
Antiquary,' true to its original habit, studying
character with a leisured observation.   Here
indeed it did not need the testimony of Scott
to prove that the supremacy of the novel was
incontestable.   The attentive reader of Fielding
must have been quite prepared to acknowledge
that the nicely distinguished shades of feeling,
the varying though similar emotions which go
to make up Oldbuck's character, could not have
been so minutely and consequently could not
have been so clearly emphasized by any dramatist
writing for the purpose of representation.   The

heart of such people the dramatist may seize, but their detail must of necessity escape him. Yet it is not perhaps in this department, where the supremacy of the novel is unquestioned, and where Scott has given instance after instance of its capacity, that he shows most conclusively his mastery over the resources of his medium. Rather is it in those departments which more particularly belong to the drama, in which the novel is not pre-eminent and can achieve at best but a secondary success. The success of the Waverley Novels, where success had long before been won, however remarkable for its magnitude, was only additional proof of the known capacities of the novel; their constant success in departments into which the novel had rarely ventured, or had ventured only to fail, was undoubtedly proof of a new capacity, and proof of such a kind as gravely to influence the subsequent course of imaginative literature. In the Waverley Novels, and for this alone they are a landmark in the history of English Literature, the province of the drama was seriously invaded. In them, the novel proved itself to be capable of dealing, not perfectly, yet excellently well, with dramatic situations, with those actions of which it had long been thought it was the peculiar province of the drama to speak. It was natural that Scott's success, his demonstration of the various resources of his medium, should have led attention away from the drama and directed it to the novel, and even those who question the gain of the result,—the preponderating influence on imaginative literature which the novel now exerts—must confess their surprise at what in his hands it was made to do.

To open many of his novels is to see on the first page how much the older imaginative form had taught him. Novelists for the most part formerly were content to work their way gradually into their story. The first book of 'Tom Jones' is described as containing "as much of the birth of the foundling as is necessary or proper to acquaint the reader with in the beginning of this history": the first chapter as "the Introduction to the work or Bill of Fare to the feast": and the second chapter as "A short description of Squire Allworthy, and a fuller account of Miss Bridget Allworthy his sister." There was no reason why the tale should have begun otherwise. An author who sets out to tell his story in narrative form, has ample time

to make his effects; he is not bound as a dramatist
is bound to catch the fancy of his audience at
once, he is under no artistic compulsion to open
with an effective situation, and consequently,
since it is always difficult to plunge *in medias
res*, or having plunged to return, he was generally
content not to do so. But many of Scott's
openings are effective in the extreme; even in
'The Antiquary,' where, if we leave the story of
Lord Glenallan out of account, there is little to
show the influence of the drama, the opening is
far more effective than was common with his
predecessors. With the meeting of two apparently chance acquaintances many a comedy
has been introduced to the stage. Even more
dramatic is the opening of 'Old Mortality'; by
the time Morton has won the prize of the popin-
jay our interests are enlisted in his favour, and
the story continues as it has begun, hurrying us
along through a series of dramatic incidents till
the hero arrives at his uncle's house.

Though it may be said that 'Old Mortality'
begins with a truly dramatic excellence, the
same cannot be pretended if we date the beginning from the actual introduction, which, while
distinguished by conformity with the title, has

no other connection with the novel. In his other books Scott has many of those introductions, in which he plays round the actual business of commencing with all the prolixity of an older school. The whole business of Jedediah Cleishbotham and Dr. Dryasdust was part of the machinery of the man. These puppets caught his fancy on its peculiar side : they were to him what a doll is to a child, or a child to an octogenarian, and of what in reality was but a simple jest he never seems to have tired. It requires, however, so I think one must confess, an abnormal perception of humour to be always as delighted with those playful excursions as Scott evidently always was. A joke that is not particularly subtle, that depends on the subterfuge of saying that the author did not write the book, but that it was taken down by some chance acquaintance of my landlord, my school-master, or my antiquary, exhausts its possibilities in less than a hundred pages, or a dozen repetitions. We may consider it, if we choose, as the mere getting under weigh, the traditional apology of " the veracious chronicler," but it differs from the initial detail of Defoe or Fielding in the fact that it never deceives. At times it has so little

ingenuity that it even irritates. The artist, who
prefaces 'The Bride of Lammermoor' with
pleasant chat about a sign-painter, appears to be
lacking in dignity. But Scott, even when writing
without any serviceable purpose, could not write
for long without throwing out something of
excellence, and if Jedediah Cleishbotham and
Mr. Pattieson had given us nothing else than the
picture of Old Mortality, they would have done
quite enough to excuse their rather cumbersome
gambols. The reader stumbles through a few
halting pages, to find suddenly—such curious
corners had the mind of this wonderful man—
a passage short indeed, but of such merit as to
catch the fancy of succeeding generations. In a
paragraph or two Scott paints a portrait which
has led tourists in Edinburgh to visit a grave,
and the inhabitants of Dumfries to erect a
monument.

"As I approached," Mr. Pattieson writes, "I was agree-
ably undeceived. An old man was seated upon the monument of the slaughtered Presbyterians, and busily employed
in deepening, with his chisel, the letters of the inscription,
which, announcing, in scriptural language, the promised
blessings of futurity to be the lot of the slain, anathematized
the murderers with corresponding violence. A blue bonnet
of unusual dimensions covered the grey hairs of the pious

I

workman. His dress was a large old-fashioned coat of the coarse cloth called hoddin-grey, usually worn by the elder peasants, with waistcoat and breeches of the same; and the whole suit, though still in decent repair, had obviously seen a train of long service. Strong clouted shoes, studded with hobnails, and *gramoches* or *leggins*, made of thick black cloth, completed his equipment. Beside him fed among the graves a pony, the companion of his journey, whose extreme whiteness, as well as its projecting bones and hollow eyes, indicated its antiquity. It was harnessed in the most simple manner, with a pair of branks, a hair tether, or halter, and a *sunk*, or cushion of straw, instead of bridle and saddle. A canvas pouch hung around the neck of the animal, for the purpose, probably, of containing the rider's tools, and anything else he might have occasion to carry with him. Although I had never seen the old man before, yet from the singularity of his employment, and the style of his equipage, I had no difficulty in recognizing a religious itinerant whom I had often heard talked of, and who was known in various parts of Scotland by the title of Old Mortality."

The critic who proposes to remark on the novel which is prefaced by the description of this personage is met at the outset by a discussion of historical interest. Happily, since for a task of this kind, literary critics are seldom competent, it is possible to avoid the issue. That novels dealing with the past must necessarily be open to the praise or objections of historians may at once be conceded, as also that there will always

be those who will consider strict historical
accuracy of vital importance. Yet for those
who allow that a legitimate distinction may be
drawn between a production which is primarily
a historical novel, and a production which is not
so much an attempt to reanimate history or to
revivify a reign, as a work of imagination de-
veloped on a historical background, the merits
of 'Old Mortality' will appear somewhat independent of the truth about the Covenanters.
In such a book as 'Quentin Durward,' which
derives most of its interest from the figure of
Louis, there is an obligation not to be false to
the spirit of the facts. In ' Old Mortality,' much
more openly a work of the imagination, the
obligation is more lightly felt. Even from a
historical novel it is possible in this respect to
ask too much. An author is not bound to
satisfy unreasonable expectations. Yet one can
imagine a reader of 'Quentin Durward' expecting
that the picture of Louis should be drawn with
literal accuracy, at the same time that one
acknowledges that it is only the most naïve who
have no suspicion in reading ' Old Mortality ' that
the author may occasionally have been tempted
to make his moving mob of enthusiasts more

picturesque than was warranted by the facts. If then Scott in 'Old Mortality' has dashed in the background of his tale in more vivid colours than the historian will approve, we have no cause to quarrel with him on that account, and if not, if he has given us a picture of literal accuracy, he has given us more than in 'Old Mortality' we had a right to expect. Of course, had he given us, instead of a picture of the Covenanters, who take up so large a space in his book, a mere caricature of them, the case would be different, but I do not think this has ever been pretended, and if in the body of the novel excessive weight is laid on their extravagances, ample amends are made at the close when Macbriar is condemned by the Council in the presence of Morton and Claverhouse. And here Scott's excellence is not merely that he puts into the mouth of his sombre fanatic a speech glowing with rare devotion to principle, but that he brings Morton and Claverhouse forward to give their differing testimony.

"The Council broke up, and Morton found himself again in the carriage with General Grahame.

"'Marvellous firmness and gallantry!' said Morton, as he reflected upon Macbriar's conduct; 'what a pity it is

that with such self-devotion and heroism should have
been mingled the fiercer features of his sect !'

"'You mean,' said Claverhouse, 'his resolution to con-
demn you to death ?—To that he would have reconciled
himself by a single text; for example, 'And Phinehas
arose and executed judgment,' or something to the same
purpose.—But wot ye where you are now bound, Mr.
Morton ?'"

By this happy juxtaposition of opinion the
author supplies his own comment.   He knew
well that however he represented the Cove- —
nanters, criticisms as divergent would continue to
be passed, and that the judgment of history was
not likely to be gravely affected by the picture
drawn of them in a work which pretended not
to the dignity of fact.

The novel which goes by the title of 'Old
Mortality' may or may not be Scott's masterpiece, but on the whole it is perhaps the one,
which, if a plebiscite of literary opinion were
taken, would obtain the largest following.   As
a novelist he has three separate claims to distinction : he can afford to be judged as a novelist
of character, as a dramatic novelist, and as a
historical novelist.   In the first capacity he
has left such a book as 'The Antiquary,' in the
second 'The Bride of Lammermoor,' and in the

third a number of productions such as 'Kenilworth,' and 'Ivanhoe,' among which it is difficult to make a selection.   But in 'Old Mortality' he puts forward all three claims at once:
as a novel of character the book may not be so
great as 'The Antiquary'; possibly as a dramatic novel it does not compete with 'The Bride
of Lammermoor,' and as a historical novel it
may be less effective than others its author has
left.   But as a novel of character it has great
claims, as a historical novel it has great
claims, and it abounds in dramatic situations.
In whatever aspect we choose to regard Scott,
whether as a historical novelist, a dramatic
novelist, or a novelist of character, we shall find
something in 'Old Mortality' to satisfy expectation, and this is no doubt the reason, and
it absolves criticism from the fruitless task of
comparison, why so many are found according
it the first place among his productions.

The mere story is exceedingly interesting, and
unlike that of 'The Antiquary,' all of a piece.
Everything is conducted in the same world of
virile events and great actions, nor is there any
attempt, as in so many of the Waverley Novels,
to make facts propitious for virtuous and un-

propitious for selfish people. From a high moral
standard—though on such a point hesitation is
becoming—the character of Mause is superior to
that of Cuddie, yet Mause is always falling into
misfortune, and the mirth-provoking Cuddie on
his feet. It will be said that it is the better
part of Cuddie, his loyalty and good-nature, that
leads him to preferment; but had Mause been
silent, the selfish prudence of her son would
have kept him from any of those dangers in
which his better part has its opportunity. All
this is in correspondence with life; in the story
not only is there nothing improbable, but there
is much that happens every day. Things fall
out unevenly—Bothwell attracts the attention
of his companions less for his courage than for
the half-credited story of his birth. Morton
refuses to tell an extremely obvious and convenient lie, and immediately his troubles begin.
Evandale by his intercession saves Morton, and
as a consequence ultimately loses his betrothed
and his life. Morton forfeits his influence among
the Covenanters because he has more wisdom
than those around him; and Balfour owes as
much of his power to the fact that he is supposed to have fought with the devil, and is

enthusiast enough to believe it, as to his proved
sagacity and strength. On the other hand, Mrs.
Wilson receives the reward of her faithful service,
Morton of his valour, Edith—for love chooses his
own rewards—of her constancy, and Jenny of
her prudence. Altogether it is the world we
live in, a basketful sufficiently surprising both
to short-sighted traders and trading moralists,
in which not all the good fruit is at the top and
not all the bad at the bottom. The book is
crowded with men and women, with troopers
and Covenanters, with characters as diverse as
old Morton and young Morton, Cuddie and
Macbriar, Jenny and old Lady Margaret, Edith,
Mrs. Wilson, and Mause; it is an epitome in a
few hundred pages of Scott's world, not a fragment, but a miniature containing something of
almost everything that appears on the big
bustling stage of the Waverley Novels. If it
be urged that Scott is not generally strong in
female character, the reader of 'Old Mortality'
may point in reply to four absolutely individual
women; and even Edith, though she may not
have as strongly marked an individuality as the
rest, has a personality made sufficiently vivid by
the force of contrast. Among his hundred men

of action there can hardly be two more opposite, and yet more life-like than Claverhouse and his — most distinguished opponent.

It is true that for all this width of treatment and observation we are not taken into any peculiarly dark corners; we are in a world of action, of open air, but then this was the world to which Scott's readers were accustomed, and with which the increasing class of novel readers is still chiefly familiar; for the countryman, the trader, the member of a profession, for all those who are not thrown into the unnatural surroundings of ignorance and want it must continue the normal world. For such people, unless the impulse of charity carry them far from "the even tenor of their way," acquaintance with the darkest corners of life must be only occasional. To those who walk the middle paths, the gravest troubles are, as a rule, made apparent by the aid of the poetical imagination in such books as 'Clarissa Harlowe,' 'The Duchess of Malfi,' or 'The Bride of Lammermoor,' each of which steps beyond the ordinary sphere. It is only to the poor and wretched that violent excess and irretrievable disaster are familiar companions, and in the beginning of this century

the poor and the wretched took up but a small
portion of the thoughts of the general public.
The world to which Scott introduces us in 'Old
Mortality' is as wide as it was then convenient
for an author who wished sympathetic readers,
to deal with.   Within its limits it is a singularly
accurate reflection of actual affairs; we have a
play of light and shade, but neither of the
brightest light nor the darkest shadow.   It was
on this sober, active, and immensely real stage
that Scott found himself most at home, con-
tentedly inhabiting, as it were, a middle space
between poetry and prose.   For the world of
'Old Mortality' is no more, like that in which
the main business of 'The Antiquary' is conducted, a world of mere prose, than it is the
world of the dramatist.   Scott, real as was his
fondness for great actions, clung tenaciously to
the simpler incidents of life, and in 'Old Mortality' battles and sieges jostle with familiar
events, touches of deep feeling alternate with
matter-of-fact detail.   As a story-teller 'Old
Mortality' shows him at the top of his power,
and a whole stock of laudatory adjectives might
be expended on the construction of the novel.

If faults are to be sought for, what is evident

may be said, that the catastrophe itself—the
appearance of Morton at Edith's window, and
her belief that she has seen a ghost—is more
theatrical, on a lower plane of imagination than
the rest, and has too little to do with the story
which it concludes. It is merely an incident;
we have no notion it is coming, and when it has
come are perhaps more surprised than pleased.
The end of 'Old Mortality,' unlike many of the
other events, has nothing inevitable about it, the
characters do not even slip towards it; the story
hangs in the clouds till an expedient is devised
by which Evandale may be got rid of, and
Edith married to Morton. If Morton was to be
brought back—and the story might well have
ended with his dismissal into space—some more
time should have been spent in giving importance to his return. Few stories are improved
by being lengthened; but one would not easily
have tired of 'Old Mortality,' nor found cause to
regret that the volume had not been closed with
a snap. A more serious criticism is that which
urges that the importance of the incidents
throughout is too great for the characters, and
tends to distract the attention from the fortunes
of Morton and Edith. But such value as this

criticism has is practical rather than theoretical.
It is difficult to say abstractly what incidents
are too large to be used for the purpose of
elucidating character, and if the effect in 'Old
Mortality' is as stated, it is a fault not so much
in the story as in its management.   The true
answer to the criticism is that for every place
where the interest of the events draws our attention away from the characters, there is another
where the events derive their interest from their
effect on the persons concerned, and that so far
is the stricture from being justified, that it is
impossible to overrate the skill with which the
narrative contrives to give a personal interest
even to occurrences of national importance. The
hero and heroine were never to Scott the exclusive points of attraction; with him they were
but two in the group of human beings to be
depicted.

Considered in this light, and without special
reference to Morton and Edith, the story of
'Old Mortality' is in every way admirable.
In itself it is interesting, and, where it is not
spun by the characters, influences them in its
course. Properly speaking, there are two classes
of incidents—those mainly of private 'and those

mainly of public interest. What is chiefly remarkable about the first, is their number and
variety: the meeting of Bothwell and Balfour in
the inn parlour; the night ride of Balfour and
Morton, and the warning of the figure at the
cross-roads; the discovery of Balfour in the loft
in one of his visionary moods, when Sharpe's
murder still occupies his thoughts; the surprise
of the family at dinner in old Morton's house;
the interview between Edith and Morton in the
dungeon; Guse Gibbie's errand; the scene where
Morton appears before Claverhouse; the trial of
Macbriar; Morton's descent upon Jenny in her
married state, with the exquisitely humorous
conversation that ensues between her and her
husband; and Morton's final interview with Balfour. Here surely—and the list could easily be
extended—is a prodigal luxury of events. Scene
succeeds scene, each as finely conceived as the
next, each striking out from the persons impli-
cated some leading trait of character, and most
of them springing naturally from the circumstances and dispositions with which the reader
is already familiar.

Of the other series of incidents, those of public
concern, it is necessary to speak more at length.

They are not so numerous.   Scott's object in writing 'Old Mortality' was not primarily to write history, and had he followed the career of Claverhouse, or Morton through the foreign wars in which he was engaged, he would at least have run the hazard of drowning the personal interest of the book. 'Old Mortality' would not have been what it is, it would have given us the figure of Claverhouse as 'Quentin Durward' gives us the figure of Louis.   As things stand there are only three incidents of public rather than private concern—the affair at Drumclog, the siege of Tillietudlem, and the battle of Bothwell Bridge. It will be of interest to consider them from two points of view. Judged as mere battle-pieces, they are sufficiently admirable to challenge comparison with Scott's poetical work in this field, but admirable as they are they suffer from the comparison.   A battle narrated in verse must always be capable of achieving higher artistic success than a battle narrated in prose, partly because the sound and tramp of the metre is better fitted to express the hurry and fever of war, but chiefly because verse is the natural medium in which to give utterance to sentiments excited to enthusiasm, and to de-

scribe events, the mere description of which
stirs the blood. It would therefore be unreasonable to expect that the battle-piece in 'Old Mortality' should affect us quite in the same way
as the account in 'Marmion' of the battle of
Flodden. Judged, however, as the central incidents in a novel, they immediately acquire a
new interest. One sees the art with which Scott
has prevented his prose description of the movements of battalions becoming tedious by reliance
on the personal element, as also how in the
same way he has bent his difficult material into
conformity with the purposes of his story. Marmion, though he plays some part in the battle
of Flodden, is not the centre of interest, for the
sufficient reason that there the poet felt he could
rely with safety on the poetical glory with which
he had invested war, on the rapid movement of
his verse, on his vivid imitation of the clash and
clang of battle. At Drumclog and Bothwell,
Scott's medium being prose, it was not possible
to do this, nor even, since he was occupied with
a novel, desirable, and consequently there he
calls our attention particularly to the very persons in whom at the time we are most interested; at Drumclog, to Claverhouse, since our

minds are still full of him, to the fate of the boy Grahame, interesting not only for his intrepidity, but for the almost paternal solicitude of his leader, and to Evandale, who, a few pages earlier, has won our affections by his chivalrous interposition in favour of his rival—and at Bothwell to Morton, and to Morton as a leader of resource and prudence. The interest of Drumclog is centred on Claverhouse, and serves to emphasize the human nature of the man whom, just before, we had seen judging like a Draco. The battle of Bothwell is lost, we are given to understand, because the Covenanters will not listen to those counsels of Morton which, by the time of the first onset, we have come to consider as the essence of political wisdom. The siege of Tillietudlem would not be what it is, were it not for the contrasted interests of Jenny and Cuddie, of Edith and her lover, and for the soldierly and avuncular figure of Major Bellenden.

If it be denied that Scott was a great artist, it will also be conceded that on such occasions the genius of his art speaks in him. To use incidents so large without sacrificing their scenic effect for the purpose of bringing into promi-

nence the humanity of a severe soldier, the
political sagacity of a youth with the nature of a
student, the simplicity of a ploughman, is indeed
to arrive somewhere near that perfection of which
Petrarch, speaking of one of Giotto's pictures,
said, *ignorantes non intelligunt, magistri autem
artis stupent*, that perfection which, though not
understood by the multitude, fills the masters of
the art with delight and despair. And what is
true of Scott here where there was most difficulty is true of him throughout the book. 'Old
Mortality' is not a tale, like so many told since
its appearance, of puppets who pass through an
infinite series of adventures, and in whom our only
interest is whether they will pass through them or
not, an interpretation of the business of fictitious
composition which though new is still surprising.
While relying on the exciting nature of his incidents, Scott continually gives evidence that he
does not rely on them alone. We are interested
in Morton before he saves Balfour, in Cuddie
and Mause before they are taken prisoners, and
in Macbriar before he is brought to the council.
Everywhere the incidents are helped by the
characters, and the characters by the incidents.

It is obvious that these are merits of a suffi-

ciently striking description, and easy to say, in
our first enthusiasm about them, that without a
story constructed somewhat after this manner, it
would be impossible for a novel to attain enduring success.   Easy to say but hard to prove, for
if it is required to show that a novel can do very
well with a narrative in one particular entirely
different, one has but to point to 'Rob Roy.'
There, certain as it is that the incidents bring
out in the most artful manner the dispositions of
the characters, the characters have hardly any
effect on the plot.   'Rob Roy' may be broadly
distinguished from 'Old Mortality' by the fact
that in it the narrative is of the most arbitrary
kind.   The reader is placed in the curious position
of becoming more or less intimately acquainted
with a set of people, about whose future actions
he can predict nothing, and who, while comport-
ing themselves as if they were

> " no other than a moving row
> Of Magic Shadow-shapes that come and go,"

give everywhere proof of their real humanity.

   With this signal exception, and allowing for
the circumstance that 'Rob Roy' is in every
sense a lighter production than 'Old Mortality,'

there are many points in common between the two books. Like 'Old Mortality,' 'Rob Roy' is a novel of character set in a historical period, and though leaning much less on history, also introducing historical characters as agents in the plot. In neither novel are hero or heroine historical and in both, while the main narrative is entirely imaginary, history is relied on to furnish the middle portion. Both stories are interesting, but Scott appears to have wearied of both, and to have finished one as hurriedly as the other. A few differences of detail serve but to emphasize the likeness, for though in dealing with the Covenanters we come freely in contact with actual facts, and in dealing with the freebooters we do not, the whole excursus on Rob Roy and his band is nothing more than a paraphrase of history. Again, though Morton's fortunes are far more intimately associated with those of Balfour, than Francis Osbaldistone's with Rob Roy's, a turn in the adventures of the respective heroes is the means of our becoming intimately acquainted with both outlaws. Far more care is expended in 'Rob Roy' than in 'Old Mortality' on the character of the heroine, so much indeed that it is one of the few novels of Scott, set in

Scotch surroundings, which does not depend to
some extent on his unusual power of depicting the humours of waiting-maids or peasant
women; against this we have to remember that
far more care is expended in 'Old Mortality'
than in 'Rob Roy' on the character of the young
hero. 'Old Mortality' is the more serious, and
perhaps when everything is considered the
greater work; the excellences of 'Rob Roy' are
not of so grave a kind, but perhaps of the two
works it is the more delightful. In both there is
a variety of moving situations and interesting
and life-like characters.

We appear to arrive at the conclusion that we
may have two novels of a somewhat similar
excellence and both admirable, even though
analysis reveals that the plot of one is natural
and the plot of the other absurd. If it is so it
will go some way to demonstrate the essential
difference between the requirements of the novel
and those of the drama. If an investigation of
the plot of 'Rob Roy' shows that to a novel it
is a matter of comparative unimportance to have
a reasonable or connected story, provided only
that it is such as to sustain the interest of the
reader, and to give opportunity to the characters,

something will have been done to prove that a
novelist who understands his business will regard
action not as an end in itself, but chiefly so far
as it reflects upon disposition and manner.

'Rob Roy,' it will not be denied, has in a high
degree both given pleasure and excited interest,
but though the slipshod story is eminently
characteristic of Scott, and each of its parts in
others of the Waverley Novels might find its
parallel, it would be difficult, in the whole range
of them, to match it exactly.   Francis Osbaldistone, the son of a wealthy merchant in London,
descended from an old Northumbrian family,
is seduced by the promptings of a romantic
spirit from the plain paths of mercantile prosperity.   His father, disgusted with his son's
disinclination for business pursuits, abandons the
idea of adopting him as a partner, and sends an
emissary to the north to discover which of his
nephews would be best fitted to fill the vacant
place.   Meanwhile before everything is ready for
the reception of the favoured nephew in London,
not knowing, I suppose, what to do with his
recalcitrant son, he dispatches him on a visit to
his uncle, Sir Hildebrand, at Osbaldistone Hall.
Throughout the book, the reader is kept in the

dark about many circumstances calculated to excite curiosity, and it is in consonance with the rest that no explanation should be offered of this whim of the merchant's. One thing only is certain, that Francis did not go to the north to do business already done, or to make arrangements for his successor. It is of the less consequence, as the fancy is productive of so many entrancing adventures, that we soon forget its apparent purposelessness.

On his way to Osbaldistone Hall, Francis falls in with a certain Mr. Morris, the secret messenger of business of State, and later on in the same day at a wayside inn with Mr. Robert Campbell, for under that name the notorious Rob Roy, while travelling in England, chose to disguise his identity. The traveller then arrives at his uncle's house, and makes the acquaintance of the remarkable family group assembled there—old Sir Hildebrand himself, his ward Diana Vernon, and the six sons of Sir Hildebrand as described in Diana's entertaining catalogue, Percie the sot, Thornie the bully, John the gamekeeper, Dickon the jockey, Wilfred the fool, and Rashleigh the scholar, who is also the lover and persecutor of Diana, the Jacobite agent, and general villain

of the piece.   The next incident of importance
is that Morris the traveller, having been robbed
while in company with Campbell by two dis-
guised men, one of whom addressed the other as
Osbaldistone, lays an information against his
quondam companion Francis.   While Francis is
being examined by the magistrate, Campbell
appears, and Morris, apparently intimidated by
what he says to him, agrees to drop the prosecution.   Diana, having insisted upon accom-
panying Francis to the magistrate's house, and
there meeting Rashleigh, ample scope is given
for the display of all the characters concerned.
Nevertheless the reader is puzzled.   Why, he
asks himself, is Francis accused, and why is the
prosecution abandoned?   Later on, he is told
that Rashleigh, to divert suspicion from himself,
the real culprit, had induced Morris to charge
his cousin, and had only desisted from his purpose because Diana, she being deep in the
councils of the Jacobites, had taken upon herself
the championship of the accused.   But this
explanation is insufficient for the facts, since it
supposes that suspicion was likely to rest on
Rashleigh; but if that had been so, it was likely
so to fall out when the charge against his cousin

was dropped, and of this there is no hint ; and since it also supposes that Morris either was an agent of Rashleigh[1] or Rob Roy, or at least sufficiently in the latter's power to fear him. On the first supposition there was no chance of his proceeding against Rashleigh, and thus working against the interests of his secret employer. On the second he could as easily have been terrified into remaining quiet altogether, as into abandoning the prosecution he had commenced. The only sufficient explanation for the accidental conduct of Rashleigh and Morris, would have been that Rashleigh had a spite against his cousin. But from this Scott was precluded since he had introduced this incident in his haste, before he had invented a cause of quarrel between them. The episode is faultily managed, since the reader justly expects that an incident of such a kind, brought in with so much effort, will have some bearing on the plot. He reads on expecting some consequence to arise from it, till in the rush of new adventures, he has forgotten what he expected.

[1] At the end of his career, if his dying speech can be trusted, Morris appears to have been acting as an agent of Rashleigh.

After this interesting affair the story proceeds as if it had never happened. Francis, still more enamoured of Diana, and having his curiosity piqued by some remarks she lets fall, questions Rashleigh about her. He elicits the following facts. Miss Vernon has before her the alternative of becoming a nun, or the wife of one of Sir Hildebrand's sons. It appears that she had originally been dedicated to the cloister, but that to fulfil a family contract, a dispensation had been procured from Rome, enabling her, if she preferred, to marry—Osbaldistone, Esq., son of Sir Hildebrand Osbaldistone of Osbaldistone Hall; and it appears further that she could not, one must suppose, conformably to her duty as a strict Catholic, marry any one else. In addition to this information, Rashleigh hints that there is nothing improbable in the contingency of Miss Vernon's marrying him. So disturbed is Francis at this news that he behaves rudely to Diana at dinner, takes refuge from his self-mortification in repeated libations, and becoming irresponsible, enters into a noisy altercation with Rashleigh, which he ends by striking him in the face, an insult, we are given to understand, never forgiven.

Introduced where it is, this quarrel as far as it
affects the relations of Rashleigh and Francis is
of little or no use to the plot.   Whenever afterwards Rashleigh crosses the path of the hero, his
actions, as far as they are explicable, are sufficiently explained by motives of self-interest.   On
the fortunes of the heroine it has an immediate
effect, since she having insisted on an explanation
from Francis, their first intimate interview takes
place.   From this colloquy the reader also profits,
gathering something . of the sinister influence
which Rashleigh exercises over the household.

Things then take a quieter turn, but Francis
soon finds a new cause for disturbance, from
observing two shadows against the blind of the
sitting-room which Diana inhabits.   Rashleigh
having gone some time before to London, it is
only left to young Osbaldistone to suppose that
his mistress is in communication with some
favoured lover.   Tormented with jealous sus-
picions, he finally determines to enter the room
unannounced, and make discovery for himself.
When he does so, he finds Diana alone, but a
tell-tale glove lying on the table.   A second
intimate interview takes place, in which Diana
admits that she has had a visitor, but refuses to

give any further information. While Francis is
still agitated by this avowal, she puts into his
hands a letter directed to him, and on which
the major part of the plot is made to hang.
The letter is from his father's partner, and
acquaints him that Rashleigh has betrayed his
trust, and, during the absence of Mr. Osbaldistone in Holland, absconded with a number of
papers of great value belonging to the firm.
Many of these papers were promises to pay
issued by respectable houses in Glasgow, and
sent on to Messrs. Osbaldistone and Tresham, as
security, and curiously enough (Osbaldistone and
Tresham must have been fond of this mode of
investment), representing almost the whole
available assets of the firm. The head clerk,
the letter continues, is already in Glasgow, for
the purpose of preventing the payment of the
bills, and Francis is urged to repair thither as
soon as possible. Diana then retires, and shortly
after returns with a sealed letter in a blank
envelope, on which, she says, in the last resort
he may rely, but which he is not to open till ten
days before the date fixed in Mr. Tresham's
communication, as that on which the credit of
the firm will expire. What is found out later

may be added here, that Rashleigh's object in all this was to render the house of Osbaldistone and Tresham bankrupt, not from any ill-will to them, but in order to embarrass various Jacobite Highland lairds who possessed promises to pay of theirs, which, if the great firm became bankrupt, would of course be so much waste-paper. At first Rashleigh's action looks merely spiteful, but Scott afterwards is at pains to set the reader right on this point. Nothing, he assures him, could well have been more reasonable. Rashleigh, a Jacobite agent, was merely, in the ordinary way of Jacobites, promoting the Jacobite cause. The Highland lairds, impoverished or ruined by the failure of their bank, and thus having the less to lose, would be the more willing to draw the sword in favour of the king over the water. It was no more than an ingenious and novel attempt to promote the fortunes of revolutionaries by draining their exchequer.[1] As to the meaning of

[1] An amusing commentary on this is that Scott tells us, near the end of the book, that Rashleigh had been forced to render up his spoils "by the united authority of Sir Frederick Vernon and the Scottish chiefs." One would not have suspected that the authority of the Scottish chiefs would have weighed with Rashleigh, as at the time

Diana's action there is no such pleasing certainty. The letter, we subsequently discover, was addressed to Rob Roy, and probably, though we have to find this out for ourselves, contained an order to him to obtain the papers if he did not possess them already, and hand them back to Francis. That Diana should conceal from Francis the contents of a Jacobite letter was a caution which explains itself. The reason for the mystery of the address is less obvious. In any case it was a secret that could not long be preserved, nor will the supposition that she meant her lover to rely on his own efforts first, serve as a full explanation, for by the time he had reached Glasgow, the scene of operations, he was free, in obedience to her instructions, to open the concealing envelope. However, when an author is writing off the reel he is not altogether to be blamed for refusing to be explicit.

Possessed of this document, Francis sets off immediately for Glasgow, and once arrived there the adventures become so fast and im-

---

he took the papers he must have contemplated their anger.

probable, that if criticism were to attempt to discuss them, tedium would be outdone. On his arrival he goes to church, and receives a mysterious message to meet a stranger on Glasgow bridge at midnight. He obeys and meets the stranger, who, preserving his incognito, and ways of mystery, leads him at length to the door of a prison; Francis excusably insists upon an explanation, but Rob Roy still maintaining a needless caution, he waives his scruples, and consents to be conducted to a cell where he finds his father's trusted clerk Owen. Owen, on making his appearance at one of the offices of his employers' correspondents in Glasgow, had opened the case to them to warn them against paying any bills which Rashleigh might present, but these merchants discovering on reference to their books that the London firm was more in their debt than they in its, determined to commit Owen, but a nominal shareholder, to prison for debt, as if that would be likely to improve their position, and as if they were not far more interested in any efforts to secure the solvency of Osbaldistone and Tresham than Owen himself was. Francis is much alarmed, and none of them can see a way out of the difficulty, when

Bailie Nicol Jarvie, a kinsman of Rob Roy's
and a trusted correspondent of Osbaldistone
and Tresham's, appears, and soon relieves the
situation. He agrees to procure Owen's release,
and to overlook the presence of Rob Roy, whom
he readily recognizes. Meanwhile, the fated time
having come, Francis opens Diana's envelope,
and the enclosure is delivered to Rob Roy, who
forthwith invites them to meet him at the Clachan
of Aberfoyle. One's first impression is that
Rob Roy's object in this invitation was the
appointment of a meeting-place where he might
safely hand over the papers after securing them
from Rashleigh. But first impressions are not
to be trusted. Next day Francis meets Rashleigh on Glasgow Green, there has a duel with
him, and is only prevented from giving him his
dispatch by the timely intervention of Rob
Roy, who is presumably interested in the pre-
servation of so active a Jacobite. It is obvious
therefore that Rashleigh had not the immediate
custody of the papers, else there was nothing to
prevent their being handed over to Francis
there and then. But also it is equally obvious
that if Rob Roy ever came to know where they
were concealed, he must either have had his

knowledge from Rashleigh, or have known on his own account where they were. And so for the further delay in their delivery, one is still as far as ever from understanding the reason. Granted that Rob Roy desired to conceal his part in the matter, granted that the papers were not in Glasgow, granted ever so many other conceivable things, it must still have been possible, if it is possible to think seriously on the subject at all, for the man who could pass two days in that city, unknown, to send a messenger with them, when they were procured, to Francis' lodging.

The next morning Francis sets out, still with no clue to their hiding-place, for the Clachan of Aberfoyle, and there, the moment he arrives, is surrounded with difficulties. The day after he is driven about from scrape to scrape till evening falls. He has not even the good fortune to speak to Rob Roy, but just at that hour when dusk melts into darkness, while wandering dejectedly by the banks of the Forth, he is overtaken by Diana and her father. It is now her business to hand him the precious bundle, she being, one might suppose—if one might suppose anything in regard to this tale—as much

surprised as he at the unexpected meeting.
Where she procured these papers is an idle
speculation. Rob Roy in the early part of that
day had been betrayed, the latter part of it he
had spent in custody. From him, then, if she
got them at all, she must have got them the day
before, when Francis was trudging from Glasgow to Aberfoyle, thus obtaining ample time to
deposit them in safety before Francis met her
riding with them into space, and if she did not
get them from Rob Roy but from some agent
of Rashleigh's further south, what was the
object in dispatching her lover to the north
that the papers might come tumbling after him?
" The whole," as Hume says on a more serious
occasion, "is a riddle, an aenigma, an inexplicable mystery." What is worth remarking, is
that if Francis had not somehow been transported to Aberfoyle, we should have missed
some of the most delightful scenes in the
Waverley Novels, scenes which secure our
interest, and paint for us with amazing skill the
varieties of Highland character.

These scenes completed, we are no nearer the
conclusion. Francis' father has got his papers,
and is again a rich man, Diana's second lover

L

turns out to have been her Jacobite father in
hiding, but before her there is still the alternative of marrying a son of Sir Hildebrand, or
entering the cloister. The long-spun Highland
episode has not brought the lovers an inch
nearer the desired consummation. If Diana
could contemplate marrying Francis now, she
could have contemplated marrying him when he
was at Osbaldistone Hall. Attentive to these
difficulties, and determined to make amends for
his past dilatoriness, Scott sets himself manfully to
the business of sweeping away the chief obstacles.
In a chapter or two he kills five of Sir Hildebrand's sons, afflicts Sir Hildebrand with a fatal
illness, and makes Rashleigh turn traitor, so
that he may be disinherited and Francis put in
his place. Shortly afterwards Sir Hildebrand
dies, and Francis Osbaldistone, now a man of
property, takes up his residence at the seat of
his ancestors. There he finds Diana and her
father in hiding, but makes no progress in his
suit. Rashleigh, who has become an agent of
the Hanoverian Government, appears suddenly
on the scene to arrest them all for high treason,
only to be quickly followed by Rob Roy, who
runs his sword through him, and thus disposes

of the possibility of the Pope's dispensation being regularly filled up.   Sir Frederick Vernon and his daughter depart for the continent, Vernon being apparently too jealously fond of her to look with favour on her lover.   But he too pays the penalty of interference with a masterful plot; he is not expected, we are told, to survive, for many months, a lingering disease. The Pope's dispensation is now the only remaining difficulty, but Scott is weary of difficulties.   It all arranged itself somehow.   " How I sped in my wooing, Will Tresham," says Francis Osbaldistone, " I need not tell you. You know too how long and happily I lived with Diana."

On the turns, surprises, and many absurdities of this story it is not necessary to remark; its very shortcomings are instructive, for though a play founded on ' Rob Roy,' and relying on the interest it has excited, may occasionally amuse an audience of novel readers, an original drama with such a plot would be fore-doomed to failure. The action, dramatically considered, is fatally faulty, everywhere the occurrences are accidental, and, till the end, leave the position of the leading actors unaltered.   The same narrative in a novel

is open to the same criticism, but strangely enough
it does not provoke it. Not one out of ten of the
readers of 'Rob Roy' can ever have troubled
himself with explaining its contradictions and
improbabilities. The reason is fairly obvious.
In a novel one thinks not of the plot but of the
characters, and conundrums that would force
themselves on the attention of an audience in a
theatre, pass almost unnoticed by the readers of
fictitious tales. It is not pretended that 'Rob
Roy' does not to some extent suffer from whatever there is in it of the ridiculous. People are
to be judged by their conduct, and even Diana
is not a more life-like figure, because she
descends more than once like a goddess from a
creaking machine; what is plain is that 'Rob Roy'
survives its story. Scott seizes on each situation
as it occurs, and makes it so absorbing and
delightful, that in watching the play of emotion
we forget altogether to ask how the circumstances responsible for it managed to happen.
Indeed his triumph with 'Rob Roy' is little
short of marvellous. The narrative with its
generally purposeless mystery was just such as
would have suited Mrs. Radcliffe. How she
would have expanded the character of the

shadowy Morris, with what dark colours she would have imbued Diana's secret assignations in the library, how the arras would have shaken, and with what delight would she have insisted on the awful alternative which lay before the heroine! But Scott is not the least disturbed by his melodramatic surroundings: he swings out into the open air; and sealed missives, mysterious meetings, and Jacobite intrigues do not prevent Diana from laughing, Andrew Fairservice from meddling, the Osbaldistones from hunting, or the sun from shining. The chief effect of the melodramatic plot, and in its way it is a suffi-ciently disastrous one, is the production of Rashleigh, a schemer of idle schemes, and much too obviously appointed to do any villainy that may need to be done.

With the exception of Rashleigh, as also with that of Sir Frederick Vernon, a faint Radcliffian figure, all the characters are real people. The whole colony at Osbaldistone Hall, Andrew Fairservice, Bailie Nicol Jarvie (though these two have more than a touch of a caricature one would not willingly exchange for reality), Dougal, and Rob Roy, all these are excellent pieces of character-painting, the chief of them

owing a great part of their excellence to the
skill with which they are thrown into circumstances in which it is easy to get at their
essence. Had Andrew Fairservice remained at
Osbaldistone Hall, he would have been but a
Scotch gardener; had Bailie Nicol Jarvie sat in
his counting-house, he would have been but a
Glasgow bailie; and even Rob Roy, had we not
seen him walking about Northumberland in
knee-breeches, would not have shown to the
same advantage on his " native heath."

The character which at once rises most superior
to its circumstances, and is best displayed by
them, is that of Diana Vernon. She is in the
thick of almost all of melodrama there is in the
plot, and yet, though taking full advantage of
each situation, she remains true to the friendly
nickname of Heath-blossom which Justice Inglewood bestows on her. The first meeting between
the lovers is conceived in the happiest vein.
Diana appears in the hunting-field, in her element, the morning, moving with all the zest
of youth, and enjoying, as only young blood
can enjoy, the gaiety of motion. The course of
the chase brings her across the path of Francis
the traveller, who, drawing his rein, has, as he

tells us, "a full view of her uncommonly fine
face and person, to which an inexpressible
charm was added by the wild gaiety of the
scene, and the romance of her singular dress
and appearance." And no doubt it is this, the
wild and romantic nature of the scenes in which
she is found, that gives throughout the book
such an inexpressible charm to the figure of
Diana. The plain fact of her position, the only
lady in Sir Hildebrand's household, and thus
thrown perforce into close companionship with
members of the opposite sex, has all the interest
of novelty. To depict a hoyden, to give a
boy a girl's name and desires, has never been
difficult, but to depict a girl who has every
temptation to become a hoyden, and who, while
sufficiently alive to them to be induced to adopt
a manner more frank than ordinary, yet remains
characteristically feminine, is a matter of the
utmost difficulty.

Diana, as long as she is in the open, and in
company with her cousins, has grace indeed, still
it is that kind of rollicking grace which alone
was possible in the circumstances. To her, as
Scott is at pains to convince us, this boyish
rush of high spirits was not natural, but due

partly to the influence of her surroundings, and partly to her desire to escape, by participating in the ways of others, from herself. Consequently when she is alone with her lover, there is none of it, or only that capacity for it, which the strictest will allow to be consistent with maidenly modesty. The Diana who appears in the library has the same high-strung temperament as the Diana who appears in the hunting-field or in the hall of Inglewood's house; all that Scott takes from her is that exuberance of health which in moments of action has its natural play. Charming as Diana is on her first appearance, she becomes infinitely more charming when we discover that her gaiety is not merely the freedom of youth without a care, but the careless sallies of a spirit kept continually in a state of high tension. No doubt all really high-spirited people, all people whose spirits are sufficiently fervent to break out in a bewitching liveliness, are also capable of responding with vivacity to the deeper emotions, but to the imaginative artist there is no more complicated task than to show this, to touch delicately the shading on the surface, while revealing the depth of feeling beneath. As to how this may be done, it is no

part of the critic's business even to venture a
suggestion. In his own way Scott achieves it,
using for his purpose a series of contrasted
incidents, and so admirably that the figure
with which he presents us, compares for truth
to nature with Thackeray's masterly portrait
in 'Esmond.' Of the two women, Beatrix is
the more dazzling, and her gaiety, since more
feminine and less boisterous, even more attractive, but she is not more life-like. If Beatrix
has had the whole world at her feet, Diana
has had half the world at hers; nor must it
be forgotten that if Scott here comes near
Thackeray's excellence, he comes near it at the
expenditure of far less trouble. Diana produces
her effect more quickly than Beatrix, because
wherever she appears she makes her effect. She
is seen in a greater variety of situations: a few
sharp strokes from the master, and a new
characteristic of his sunny creation slips out
in response to the altered scene. We first meet
Diana in the flush of her youth, and at our first
meeting with her, we see, conformably with
Scott's custom with all his greater characters,
nothing more than the outside. She appears
next as the chivalrous friend of her unfriended

cousin, a transition with nothing of violence
in it, as happy youth is prone, if it is prone
to anything besides its own development, to
generous impulses; then, when we feel we owe
her a debt of gratitude, as justly indignant.
Let those who doubt Scott's insight as an
artist study that chapter of 'Rob Roy,' when
Diana, who has called Francis to her to reproach
him for his conduct, throws open, in her generous
frankness, the troubled places of her mind, or
that other chapter when, almost surprised of her
secret, and with every excuse for anger at her
lover's intrusive curiosity, she brings her quick
wit to his aid. As commentaries on Diana's
character, these scenes would have lost half
their value had the way not been prepared for
them. As it is, their contrast with those that
have preceded is singularly impressive: we
believe in Diana's seriousness because we believed in her mirth. Melodramatic perhaps both
chapters are: let us prefer to consider what
purposes the melodrama is made to serve. But
Scott's real triumph is, when near the close of
the book he shows us his heroine in an attitude
of unexpected tenderness, unexpected when it
comes, I mean, but coming with such force

that when it has come we are ready to declare
that all along we had expected it. Diana, in
company with her father, has overtaken Francis
Osbaldistone on the road, and delivered the
fateful packet.

"'In the attitude,' says her lover, 'in which she bent
from her horse, which was a Highland pony, her face,
not perhaps altogether unwillingly, touched mine—she
pressed my hand, while the tear that trembled in her eye
found its way to my cheek instead of her own. It was a
moment never to be forgotten—inexpressibly bitter, yet
mixed with a sensation of pleasure so deeply soothing
and affecting, as at once to unlock all the flood-gates of
the heart. It was *but* a moment, however ; for, instantly
recovering from the feeling to which she had involuntarily
given way, she intimated to her companion she was ready
to attend him, and putting their horses to a brisk pace,
they were soon far distant from the place where I stood.
"'Heaven knows, it was not apathy which loaded my
frame and my tongue so much, that I could neither
return Miss Vernon's half embrace, nor even answer
her farewell. The word, though it rose to my tongue,
seemed to choke in my throat like the fatal *guilty*, which
the delinquent who makes it his plea knows must be
followed by the doom of death. The surprise—the
sorrow, almost stupefied me. I remained motionless
with the packet in my hand, gazing after them, as if
endeavouring to count the sparkles which flew from the
horses' hoofs. I continued to look after even these had
ceased to be visible, and to listen for their footsteps long
after the last distant trampling had died in my ears. At
length, tears rushed to my eyes, glazed as they were by

the exertion of straining after what was no longer to be
seen. I wiped them mechanically, and almost without
being aware that they were flowing, but they came thicker
and thicker. I felt the tightening of the throat and
breast, the *hysterica passio* of poor Lear; and, sitting
down by the wayside, I shed a flood of the first and
most bitter tears which had flowed from my eyes since
childhood.'"

It is perilously near nonsense, of course;
Diana had no business to be galloping about
by the side of the Forth, but what nonsense it
is; was ever romance so delightful?

Of all Scott's numerous qualities this capacity
for pure romance at the age of forty-five was
not the least remarkable, for though great
imaginative work has been done. in age, it is
seldom imaginative work of this sort. The
imagination of a man of middle life, however
active, is almost invariably serious; it is not, as
the imaginative fancies of youth so often are, the
mere play of the mind. With most responsible
people the purely romantic vein, which takes
delight in conceiving generously improbable
actions, runs thin quite soon. It is remarkable
then that in almost all Scott's novels there
should be observable a strong vein of irresponsible romance, and that, if anything, it

should be most observable in his later productions.   Even his novels of character are not free
from it.   In 'Rob Roy' it appears everywhere,
in 'Guy Mannering' it supplies a motive to the
novel, in 'The Antiquary,' where what is good
is extremely staid, it runs riot in the story of
Lord Glenallan, and 'The Heart of Midlothian'
becomes at the end just such a tale as children
tell to themselves to beguile the time away.

   To preserve one's youth, said Mr. Arnold, is
the secret of genius, and there is a freshness in
these enthusiastic bursts of fancy of which we
are apt to feel the fascination.   But though
where, as in 'Rob Roy,' they form part of the
essence of a book, they are not to be taken
too seriously; in other cases where, as in 'The
Antiquary' or 'The Heart of Midlothian,' the
romantic part is out of harmony with the rest,
the consequent detriment to the novel is evident.
'The Antiquary' may be defined as a novel
of character into which is foisted a tale of
diablerie.   To fit a definition to 'The Heart
of Midlothian' is not so easy.   Perhaps the
most famous of Scott's works, it begins in one
manner, continues in another, and ends in a
third.   If it is to be considered as a whole, and

certainly, if attention is to be directed to its excellence, it is, like 'The Antiquary,' a novel of character. All that is good in it, is of that kind of effort which an imaginative genius of mature years might be expected to find congenial. The odd thing is that, though appearing just two years before 'Ivanhoe,' what portion of it is historical is managed with less art than was usual with Scott, and that, though published in the same year as 'Rob Roy,' when it wanders into the region of romance, it fails. While one is at a loss to discover reasons for the first defect, the second is explicable enough. It was too late, when Scott thought of it, to turn 'The Heart of Midlothian' into a fairy tale, and though the sketches of Sir George and Lady Staunton are not above the capacity of very ordinary novelists, and the discovery of the long-lost heir in circumstances visiting the sins of the fathers upon the children is an incident as highly coloured as commonplace, it is probably true that no excellence could have saved this part of the book. Long before Effie appears as a leader of fashion we have come to accept the cow-feeder and his daughters as part of the natural order; we have become accustomed to the distresses of birds of very ordinary plumage, and are in no humour to see them decked out in peacock's feathers. Jeanie Deans and her father in prosperity lose half their charm, nor is the matter mended with the attempt at a compromise between this flight of genial fancy and the essential tragedy of the story. One would not willingly decide that the result is a *dénouement* which is an error in taste, but it comes as near it as it was possible for Scott to come.

As to the beginning of the book, coming from whom it did, it is an enigma. In a superlative degree Scott had the art of combining the historical and fictitious occurrences in a narrative. To his success in this particular, 'Old Mortality' bears emphatic witness, and it would be simple to furnish the curious reader with a dozen other instances as strong, yet 'The Heart of Midlothian' begins with as plain a piece of history as has ever opened a novel. Had Scott been working here according to his usual method, the tale would have begun by introducing us to some of the chief characters and circumstances, and the narrative of the Porteous riots, as far as it concerned Robertson, Butler, and Effie, would

have been incorporated later. As it is, we have
the history before we have reason to take interest
in it, and when in the eighth chapter we come
effectively in contact with the chief actors, we have
to take a long step backward in time. I do not
know whether this last defect in construction has
weighed heavily with the readers of 'The Heart
of Midlothian,' but what would be thought of a
dramatist who began his second act at a period
anterior to his first! A novel is not exacting in
point of narrative, but some demands it must
make. It may be reasonably asked of a novelist
that whatever atmosphere he places us in, whether
a sordid, a real, or a romantic one, that atmosphere should be preserved throughout. An
equally modest request is that which asks that
a fictitious tale should be fictitious, and such
facts as are introduced subservient to the purpose
of the story. It is not required of a novel that
it should have a more reasonable narrative than
'Rob Roy,' any more than it is required that it
should not narrate the battles of Drumclog or
Bothwell Bridge, but the irreducible minimum
of requirement is that it should neither end nor
begin as 'The Heart of Midlothian' is begun
and ended.

Between the beginning and ending, neither of which is artistically successful, is sandwiched the vital part of the book. But even here, where there is so much to praise, there is a difficulty in the way of unrestricted laudation. One of the most famous of novels, 'The Heart of Midlothian,' is also one of the most uncomfortable. Not only does a moral run through it, but we are asked to make the application. " Reader," says Scott at the end, with a manly disregard of the canons of his art, "this tale will not be told in vain, if it shall be found to illustrate the great truth, that guilt, though it may attain temporal splendour, can never confer real happiness; that the evil consequences of our crimes long survive their commission, and like the ghosts of the murdered, for ever haunt the steps of the malefactor: and that the paths of virtue, though seldom those of worldly greatness, are always those of pleasantness and peace." Alas for the austerity of morals that will not quite permit of such facility of illustration. The good man, say the philosophers from Plato to Paley, is happy, and the bad man miserable. We must believe, if we can, that the rule is without spiritual exceptions, but to give it a material application

M

is to put faith to a trial. Happy doubtless was
Socrates quaffing his hemlock, unhappy, let us
suppose it, Nero fiddling, but had Effie Deans
been hanged, where would have been the peace
of mind of her sister, and had Lady Staunton
not found her son, what would have happened
to dash the fashionable pleasures in which she
and her husband took delight? In every great
imaginative work, as wherever human beings
are found, side lights will be thrown upon morals,
but the moral insight we gain is derived not
from the conduct of events, but from a study of
the dispositions of the characters. The fictitious
story being entirely at the writer's mercy, nothing
can be more idle than that he should refer to its
authority.

But though thus the actual moral appended
to 'The Heart of Midlothian,' like that which
Coleridge plaintively subjoins to his delightful
lines on the Raven, may be put aside, it is not
possible to speak so lightly of the didactic teaching of the book. It is quite obvious, I think,
that Scott meant, as he would probably have
expressed it, "to kill two birds with a stone," or,
in other language, to write a readable novel, and
to promote the cause of abstract virtue. The

story will entertain, we may suppose him to have
said, but its reader will have to accept my dogma
that in no circumstances is it possible to permit
of any deviation from the truth. There is a
quaintness in this, of course, coming from the
placid denier of the authorship of The Waverley
Novels which it is difficult to miss, but that is
an antique fallacy of argument, and Scott puts
his proposition so seriously that it would be dis-
courteous to avoid it. A novel of the moral
problem order cannot reasonably be expected
to press a point of accepted morality, since if it
did it would be pardonably accused of being
dull. There is nothing then to complain of in
the fact that Scott's dogma will not fit with the
practice of honest men. Laws are changed
frequently in civilized communities because it is
found that they have grown so out of consonance
with an advancing moral sense that juries will
rather perjure themselves daily than give effect
to them. And perhaps it may be said that few
articles of any modern church are altered, till
the majority of its members have formed the
habit of explaining them away. What is to be
complained of is that ' The Heart of Midlothian,'
being a novel, should raise just the question it

does, on which, though most men are vaguely
agreed, few care to formulate a definite opinion.
How much simpler the world would be if such
a thing as lying had never been invented it is
needless to speculate. The business of courts
of criminal justice would be reduced to putting
one question and receiving one answer, and the
labour of historians sensibly diminished. Still,
the world being as it is, and the invention made,
it has seemed and does seem that there are
occasions in practice in which the immediate disaster brought about by stating the fact, outweighs
the theoretical advantage. What Royalist in
whose house the fugitive Charles had been concealed would have hesitated to answer a leading
question in the negative? how different the impression made by Desdemona had she informed
upon Othello. The poets, we may be sure, have
not written variations on the phrase *splendide
mendax* for nothing. With all this, however, these
cases are so rare, and it is always so difficult to
persuade men of the necessity of truth-speaking,
that the weakness of human nature prefers not
to contemplate them. Against this weakness,
no doubt, it is the duty of ethical writers to
wage war; it was the office of casuistry to test

the sweeping generalizations of morals, as it is
the fancy of Ibsen to-day, by opposing one moral
axiom to another, to arouse activity on ethical
subjects.   As moralists, and every one in so far
as he is not an automaton is a moralist, we
ought rather to welcome than to avoid such discussions; we ought even to welcome a discussion
on this particular subject, on which, if on any,
a man would desire to speak guardedly.   But as
novel readers we may fairly ask that we should
not be given the alternative either of accepting
offhand a generalization which we are unwilling
to accept, or of giving offhand a denial to a
proposition to which exception is only to be
taken with caution.   The interests of truth,
especially in a modern world where ' other
interests are losing their weight, every one has
at heart, and since most men would, if they
could, rather write an ethical treatise than be
found tripping on such a subject, the novelist
who demands an opinion from an arm-chair on
the general question of truth is safe to irritate
his readers.

On the larger issue of the advisability of dis-
cussing moral questions in fiction, it ought not
to be necessary to say much.   Admitting the

weakness of human nature, and it seems to me that in theoretical discussions we are too apt to neglect it, it must also be admitted that though men ought to find ethics of sufficient interest in themselves, they are not likely to do so. In the great movement for the abolition of the slave trade in the southern portion of the United States, 'Uncle Tom's Cabin' exercised an influence equal to that of a hundred pamphlets, and the view recently emphasized by Mr. Grant Allen, that a "verse may find him who a sermon flies," is too obvious to be disputed. Still, as a writer is hardly likely to find success at one time as a theologian and a poet, so novelists who choose to turn their novels into essays have much against them when it comes to a question of artistic merit. It will not unusually happen that their own attention is distracted from their characters, and as long as the question is alive,[1] their readers will have something else to think of than the truth of nature. Even Scott, though he has escaped the first danger, falls a victim to the second. We

[1] As long as the question is alive, since I imagine that a Greek religious problem would not seriously interfere with the artistic interests of a modern reader of a Greek play.

find ourselves thinking not of Jeanie Deans, but of her situation.

For the faults of a writer of such eminence there will always be found apologists, and it may be replied to the foregoing argument, that the mere fact of an imaginative author having a moral intention is not in itself sufficient to destroy the artistic effect, and that where the moral is found to intrude, it is as often to be blamed to the reader as to the writer.   Suppose, for example, the apologists may say, Shakespeare had really written ‘Macbeth’ to make murder more odious still, or Hamlet to prove—to give an extravagant instance—that a poisoner should receive his dispatch when he is

> “about some act
> That has no relish of salvation in’t,”

these plays would remain just what they are. ‘Macbeth’ and ‘Hamlet’ would still be two of the greatest tragedies in the world, even supposing one had been written to give Shakespeare's testimony where even Shakespeare's testimony was not needed, and the other to extend his sanction to the suggestions of superstitious ferocity; and if this be so, our apologists may

continue, why should Scott provoke cavil by
doing what Shakespeare may have done? Surely
the scruples of Jeanie Deans, provided they
furnish the artist with a variety of interesting
situations, and opportunity to study a heart torn
with conflicting emotions, are as good a subject
for imaginative treatment as the foibles of Oldbuck, the indecision of Morton, or the schemes
of Rashleigh Osbaldistone. The answer is to
be found in an examination of the instances.
Allowing for a moment the supposition that
Shakespeare's intentions were as represented, it
is to be remarked that we are not troubled with
them. When Hamlet gives utterance to his
vindictive meditations, the reader does not pause
to think of their moral complexion, his attention
is wholly occupied with considering the curious
convolutions of a mind that could snatch, as a
cause for delay, at a notion so alien to its
character. So in reading 'Macbeth,' where one
deed of blackness is hustled upon another, nothing is further from our thoughts than the
criminal law. Granted that Shakespeare's intentions were as stated, De Quincey laid his
finger on the miracle of the masterpiece when
he said that the play is so contrived that our

sympathy, "not our moral, but our intellectual sympathy," is with the usurper to the end. This is not the method of a moralist, and though of what a great artist thinks first, the wise moralist will also think, he will think of it last. Matter that is of paramount importance to ethical writers, Shakespeare, it will be found, keeps surprisingly to himself. Need it be added that in 'The Heart of Midlothian' Scott presses his moral intention with more than Shakespearian insistence?

The truth is that in selecting the story of Helen Walker as the basis for a novel, Scott went out of his way to create difficulties. In the first place, though he has not attempted to tell the story without raising a moral discussion, and indeed his effort is in the opposite direction, it would not have been easy to do so. In the second place, the story though true is improbable, and in the third the course of events prevents us from feeling an uninterrupted sympathy with the heroine. It is difficult even in reading 'The Heart of Midlothian' to believe that any woman with such a warmth of sisterly affection would have acted as Jeanie Deans did, nor does it avail us to be told that Helen Walker did actually act in precisely that manner, since there

are many things we have to accept as facts, of
too rare occurrence for the purposes of fiction.
Facts are but isolated truths, but fiction aims
at the truth of nature. I suppose that the
Admirable Crichton may have acted just as he
is said to have acted, yet Ainsworth has done
something to show that he makes an impossible
hero for a novel. It is difficult to believe in
Jeanie Deans' chief action, and this difficulty of
belief chills sympathy at once. When we do
believe, our sympathy is not active. The Roman
who condemned his son to death acted from a
sense of what justice required, yet we should
consider that the demands both of ethics and
humanity had been satisfied had the gods
suddenly turned him to stone to stand in the
market-place as a witness to his probity. An
author who puts forward for such actions a
claim for undivided admiration, asks too much
from humanity. Mr. Stevenson, one of the
most exquisite of artists, understood the philosophy of the matter when he proposed to assign
such an act as the judicial condemnation of a
son to a rugged and brutal character.[1] From

[1] 'Weir of Hermiston' remains a fragment, but it is
doubtful if Mr. Stevenson would have carried out his

'Weir of Hermiston' we should have welcomed
it. A far flight of virtue it would have appeared
for his "clay carcass" to aspire to. It is different
when we are asked to consider a similar action
coming as the fine flower of an unblemished life.
In these affairs of the imagination the judgment
is always comparative, and where the virtue has
no blackness to set it off, but claims approval
for itself, we pause to analyze our sensations.
Concerning the case of Jeanie Deans they are
hopelessly divided : on the one side, truth, on the
other, those affections on the strength of which
society depends. It would be simple to multiply
words in speaking of the beneficial agency of
the family, of

> "all the charities
> Of father, son, and brother" :

of that first school in which a man learns he
cannot live by self. There is something sus-
picious in a virtue that is at war with the best
instincts of our nature.[2]

---

intentions, he being informed that in Scotland at the
beginning of the century, no father would have been
permitted to sit in judgment on his son.

[2] The political reader is aware that the provision of the
English law excluding the evidence of husband and wife,
when one or the other is on trial, has been defended by

It is this many-sided difficulty that makes
'The Heart of Midlothian' an uncomfortable
book, but how few books contain such wonderful things, how few heroines are so drawn to the
life! Possibly, in the central and immortal part
of it there are not more effective situations than
in many other of Scott's novels. For mere
quantity and brilliancy of episode, 'Rob Roy'
will fairly compare even with 'The Heart of
Midlothian.' What it wants is the seriousness,
the dignity which comes of dealing with large
concerns, that distinguishes the greater book.
Jeanie's discovery that she is expected to give
evidence, her self-communing thereupon, and
her interview with her sister, the trial scene,
the charming interlude of the parting between
Dumbiedykes and Jeanie, that graver one when
Madge tells her "sad tales" on the road to
London, and the final interview with the Queen,
these are incidents that have become part of
every reader's experience; and they have become
so, not because they are links in a chain of

---

reasoning similar to the above. May we see in the proposal to get rid of the provision altogether, the advancing
claims of the State even when they are opposed to those
of family?

exciting events, but because taken all together they serve to unfold a story of an essentially human interest.

Of three of these incidents, the trial scene, the meeting with Madge Wildfire, and the interview with Queen Caroline, it is impossible to speak adequately. They must be left, like much of Shakespeare, to make their own impression. When he comes actually to deal with Nature the critic is at a loss. A tree standing out sharply from the sky, "a violet by a mossy stone," the ceaseless movement of the waves, these are sights familiar enough, but which strike every observer differently. A man must give something to the outer world, for everything he receives from it; and it is in just proportion to what he brings that he will receive pleasure from these triumphs of imagination which seem Nature herself. We turn to the trial scene, and in place of what we expected to see, a harsh law administered by harsh men, we find ourselves transplanted to a period in which such laws were enacted, and, since then enacted, not then appearing as they appear to us now. We are no modern spectators passing censure lightly on bygone cruelties, but members of the audience listening, with our hearts in our mouths, to the kindly judge pronouncing doom. We become, if the figure is not too startling, ourselves people of the past, and open our eyes with a start, as we might awake from a vivid dream, to find our own world unfamiliar. "Young woman," said the judge, "it is my painful duty to tell you, that your life is forfeited under a law, which, if it may seem in some degree severe, is yet wisely so, to render those of your unhappy situation aware what risk they run, by concealing, out of pride or false shame, their lapse from virtue." To understand the genius required to write that passage, is to have some idea of the insight which enabled Scott to see, behind the historical changes in customs and conventions, the real identity of men.

But if Scott is like Shakespeare here,—and I cannot but think that if Shakespeare had read the trial scene he would have recognized a kindred spirit,—he is even more plainly comparable with him when he comes to write of Madge Wildfire. There no doubt his task was indefinitely difficult. Madness, the frenzy of the imagination loosed, seems especially to call for that imaginative treatment which only the

poet can give it. But beyond this, being, as
any violent disturbance of law, unpleasing, it is
especially unfitted for detailed description. If
Shakespeare's imagination seldom shows to more
advantage than when he is dealing with the
mad Ophelia, it is there also, in the short space
he has devoted to her, that we get an idea of
his tact. The successful presentments of madness in prose fiction might be counted upon one's
fingers. In his treatment of Madge Wildfire
Scott took a hint from Cervantes. As with
Don Quixote so with Madge. Till it comes
to the deathbed her vagaries provoke a smile,
and as it happens in the story of that pathetic
madman, where the lightest chord is struck
there is an undertone that is sad. In 'The
Heart of Midlothian' Madge Wildfire takes up
a large space; had every passage been as
moving as the last we should not have suffered
it. The novelist cannot afford to press his
readers as hardly as the dramatist. One gets
the contrast between Shakespeare's method and
Scott's when one remembers that while the
death of Madge is a catastrophe, the announce-
ment of Ophelia's comes to the audience as a
relief. Once or twice before that climax Scott's

madwoman breaks out into snatches of song, he thereby completing his picture, and coming as near to the truth of poetry as it is possible for prose in an essentially poetical matter to come.

"'Ay! is this Sunday?' says Madge, replying to the rebuke of her strangely selected companion. 'My mother leads sic a life, wi' turning night into day, that ane loses a' count o' the days o' the week, and disna ken Sunday frae Saturday. Besides, it's a' your whiggery—in England, folk sings when they like—and then, ye ken, you are Christiana, and I am Mercy—and ye ken, as they went on their way, they sang.'—And she immediately raised one of John Bunyan's ditties:—

'He that is down need fear no fall,
    He that is low no pride;
He that is humble ever shall
    Have God to be his guide.

Fulness to such a burthen is
    That go on pilgrimage;
Here little, and hereafter bliss,
    Is best from age to age.'

"'And do ye ken, Jeanie, I think there's much truth in that book, the Pilgrim's Progress. The boy that sings that song was feeding his father's sheep in the Valley of Humiliation, and Mr. Greatheart says, that he lived a merrier life, and had more of the herb called Heart's-ease in his bosom, than they that wear silk and velvet like me, and are as bonny as I am.'"

How lightly the whole passage runs off with that touch of imaginative insight with which it is closed.

Of the characters in this novel of character
there is little to be added to what has been so
often said. As is usual, we are introduced to a
various world. There is quite a host of sketches :
the Saddletrees, Mrs. Balchristie, Ratcliffe, Mrs.
Glass, the Duke of Argyll and Queen Caroline,
some over-coloured, but two of them, Saddletree
and the Duke, as good in their different ways of
humorous exaggeration and literal accuracy, as
any of the numerous subsidiary figures that
Scott struck out in the rapid course of his
authorship. Besides these there are at least five
characters of importance : Jeanie Deans and
Madge Wildfire; Butler, best perhaps in his
introduction, and though capable of becoming
tedious, throughout consistent; Davie Deans,
always, I think, a little tiresome, but extra-
ordinarily life-like, the one defect of both being
that they repeat themselves ; and Dumbiedykes,
too continuously food for merriment, yet ful-
filling his perennial office with a certain droll
ripe naturalness infinitely pleasing. "The fools
in Shakespeare," says Hazlitt, who never said a
foolish thing, "are of his own or nature's making."
It is the same with the fools in Scott. He too
"had hardly such a thing as spleen in his com-

position." There was never a foible that his heart was not large enough to tolerate, or a folly he had not humorous sympathy to understand.

In dealing with the first of these characters he had much against him, the central incident on which Jeanie's fortunes hang, by its want of human warmth, putting our interest in her to the severest test. Here was a Scotch peasant girl who was about to act in a manner unusual, prompted by motives of a highly abstract kind. How was such a character to be made interesting or lovable? To understand that we have to read 'The Heart of Midlothian.' It was not possible, of course, to make the central action very probable or very attractive, and what was not possible has not been done. On the contrary, Scott, by giving to his heroine so feminine a character, has rather heightened the original improbability of the tale. Nevertheless our interest in her, and our sympathy with her troubles, are as uninterrupted as in the circumstances they could be, and this Scott has effected by emphasizing the fact that the precisian part of Jeanie is an inheritance, and by throwing the cold weight of it, and the main responsibility for it, on her father. The heroine of 'The Heart

of Midlothian' is represented as an unusually
docile and womanly creature, upon whose nature
it was no difficult task to graft enthusiastic
principles, doubly attractive to her on account
of their masterful rigidity. Not that there is
anything artificial about her Cameronianism, it
has become a real part of her, but the Sabbatarian
who is so ready with her little sanctimonious
rebukes, the altruist who is prepared to sacrifice
everything for principle, though true to her
acquired nature, is not as true, if the expression
be allowable, to her natural nature, as the
woman who utters her despairing cry when her
father swoons in the Court, who demurely follows
Madge Wildfire, or pleads before the Queen.

This is the magic of the alchemist: he has
made his Roman sister not the least like the
Roman father of legend,—a thing of virtuous
stone,—but a creature soft, warm, and human, and
in whom, even when she makes her sacrificing
avowal, humanity cries out. And, looking at
Jeanie in this light, it was a proper thing too
that she should have been successful in her
embassy—though one can imagine how Richardson would have scorned such a *dénouement*—it
was a proper thing, as it seems, to bring out still

more effectively the main lines on which the character is built.⌡

"'I have not the least doubt,' said Argyll to Jeanie, as they were driving back in his carriage from the scene of his interview with Queen Caroline, 'I have not the least doubt that the matter is quite certain.'

"'O God be praised! God be praised!' ejaculated Jeanie; 'and may the gude leddy never want the heart's ease she has gien me at this moment—And God bless you too, my Lord! without your help I wad ne'er hae won near her.'

"The Duke let her dwell upon this subject for a considerable time, curious, perhaps, to see how long the feelings of gratitude would continue to supersede those of curiosity. But so feeble was the latter feeling in Jeanie's mind, that his Grace, with whom, perhaps, it was for the time a little stronger, was obliged once more to bring forward the subject of the Queen's present. It was opened accordingly. In the inside of the case were the usual assortment of silk and needles, with scissors, tweezers, &c.; and in the pocket was a bank-bill for fifty pounds.

"The Duke had no sooner informed Jeanie of the value of this last document, for she was unaccustomed to see notes for such sums, than she expressed her regret at the mistake which had taken place. 'For the hussy itsell,' she said, 'was a very valuable thing for a keepsake, with the Queen's name written in the inside with her ain hand doubtless—*Caroline*—as plain as could be, and a crown drawn aboon it.'

"She therefore tendered the bill to the Duke, requesting him to find some mode of returning it to the royal owner.

"'No, no, Jeanie,' said the Duke, 'there is no mistake in the case. Her Majesty knows you have been put to great expense, and she wishes to make it up to you.'

"'I am sure she is even ower gude,' said Jeanie, 'and it glads me muckle that I can pay back Dumbiedykes his siller, without distressing my father, honest man.'

"'Dumbiedykes? What, a freeholder of Mid-Lothian, is he not?' said his Grace, whose occasional residence in that county made him acquainted with most of the heritors, as landed persons are termed in Scotland—'He has a house not far from Dalkeith, wears a black wig and a laced hat?'

"'Yes, sir,' answered Jeanie, who had her reasons for being brief in her answers upon this topic.

"'Ah! my old friend Dumbie!' said the Duke; 'I have thrice seen him fou, and only once heard the sound of his voice—Is he a cousin of yours, Jeanie?'

"'No, sir,—my Lord.'

"'Then he must be a well-wisher, I suspect?'

"'Ye—yes,—my Lord, sir,' answered Jeanie, blushing and with hesitation.

"'Aha! then, if the Laird starts, I suppose my friend Butler must be in some danger?'

"'O no, sir,' answered Jeanie much more readily, but at the same time blushing much more deeply."

And this is the woman who was ready for her sacrifice. What could better exemplify the tender and confiding heart, what could be more in keeping than the whole of this trivial incident with the fantastic fitfulness of events? Every one must know, how, after the most serious occasions, occasions in which all is at the

hazard,—some life perhaps inexpressibly dear,—
and in which the rush of feeling seems to swamp
its gentler gradations, there succeeds, when the
tension is relaxed, a period in which every
sensation is on the alert, and one trembles on
the verge of divided emotions. It is then, in
this ecstatic condition, when one may either
break down, give oneself up to happy laughter,
or pass from one phase of feeling to the other,
that one's essential thoughts, the mind being
swept vacant of merely transitory impressions,
will be startlingly apparent. The world, with its
thousand interests, has for a time been forgotten,
and now when it returns upon us, what is dearest
in it will be the first to return. "'O no,'sir,'
answered Jeanie much more readily, but at the
same time blushing much more deeply." Had
she ever confessed as much to herself, before the
relief following on the success of her long
embassy had brought her secret to her lips?

And so Scott tells us with the sagest of
smiles, that after all Jeanie Deans did not live for
the fulfilment of a remorseless duty, but for the
satisfaction of " those thoughts, those passions,
those delights," which, since the weary world
began, have so charmingly tormented and en-

nobled the daughters of men.   O ! the sage and
dear master, and knew he not also, let us not
grant to it a moment's dubiety, of how little consequence is an illustration of the best of moral
axioms, of the straitest of rules to guide our
conduct of every day, when compared with what
we can learn when he shows us the movements
of the heart.

CHAPTER III

SCOTT AS A NOVELIST OF ACTION

THE writer who has a thesis to develop often finds himself in the position of having to face uncomfortable facts. Where his thesis is an old established one, and it has become a kind of maxim with the public that it is true, he will be tempted to give too little weight to whatever makes against it, and even where the fancied interests of the majority are not bound up with the case, there is nothing of which the majority is so fond as black and white. A theory that admits of seeming exceptions, that cannot be stated quite nakedly, is safe to be wanting in popular attraction. Yet it is better that it should lack this than that it should be exposed to ruin at the first whiff of sane consideration. The large proposition with which these pages open, that the sphere of the novel is that of character rather than that of action, must not be taken to express more than is said.   Already in speaking of Scott's novels of character it has been indicated that the two spheres cannot be kept distinct, and that the novelist who wishes to elucidate character fully, to display both its depth and variety, must keep in mind the importance of action.   Yet with this, as it must be admitted, it would still be possible to assert, if one cared to indulge in unattached theorizing, that the novelist who devotes his attention exclusively to action will fail.   Unfortunately for the simplicity of the present thesis, the facts will not fit with this view.   If there ever was a novel that was exclusively a novel of action, it is 'The Bride of Lammermoor;' if there ever was a successful production, it is this novel in which Scott frankly adopts the methods of the drama. Under the circumstances all that the critic may reasonably attempt to show is that what the novel achieves, it achieves with difficulty, as if about a work alien to its character, and that in some particulars it misses the highest dramatic success.

The first and last impression of the reader of 'The Bride of Lammermoor' is one of astonishment, and certainly no one who had only read Scott's poems could have suspected that he kept concealed within him, to be revealed ten years after the publication of ' The Lady of the Lake,' and of all places in a novel, such a fund of poetical feeling. Vivid as his poems are, full of martial ardour, and refined by passages of delicate description, they display nowhere the same intensity of imagination and passion, which is apparent in this romance, that occupies a place by itself among his voluminous productions. As a poet Scott has many excellences, but if his whole work be considered it will be seen that his distinguishing excellences are those of a great prose author : his novels as well as his poems, with the necessary exception of occasional passages, are the productions of a man whose genius inclined to prose rather than to poetry. With all his knowledge of the world, and of the people who compose it, with all his fondness for great actions and his admirable contempt for the trivial incidents which are the frequent stock in trade of the novelist, he had not in any degree the Shakespearian or poetical insight, he had not more than a hint of that imagination, supposed to belong peculiarly to poets, which sees beyond what is to be seen. And this is perhaps why imaginative children so often do not take kindly to Scott; his power of telling stories does not impress them as much as it ought, since if there is one thing an imaginative child can do, it is to tell itself stories all day long, and his knowledge of character does not impress them at all, because children are practically ignorant of character. They miss in him those flashes which in the poets illumine for them a world outside their own. It is true that they do not know what it is they miss, and if they are questioned will probably give the wrong reason why it happens that they so often, unlike older people, find the Waverley Novels wearisome. But it is easy to test it for ourselves. Let a boy of fourteen read 'Macbeth,' and though he will not understand it he will come under its spell; he will feel that the master is speaking to him of a world to which youth does not possess the key. To give the same boy 'Quentin Durward' is to find oneself listening to the complaint that it is dull, and perhaps also to the explanation that there is not a quick enough succession of romantic incidents. Yet as every mature reader of 'Quentin Durward' knows, there is quite sufficient incident in the novel, and what does make it go slowly is not the want of incident, but the want of the vivifying insight of the poet. The thing is a trifle laboured ; we learn all about Louis, but we learn all about him, as we should learn all about him in real life, by taking trouble, whereas the poet—we may keep to Shakespeare as the perfect instance of a man working by poetical methods— saves us trouble everywhere, he makes his effects by a few sudden strokes of the pen. Scott, simply because he is a prose author, will always be under-rated by the young, as he will always be rated at his full value, if not over-rated, by those past middle age, on whom the poetical imagination is losing its hold. Plato's apparently enigmatical proposition that poetry is a noble lie, does not seem particularly enigmatical to those who have been brought, by the tedious teaching of life, to recognize that the world, unless indeed we infuse something of ourselves into it, is a place in which predominates the colour of grey.

Possibly, to the careful observer, the qualities that make Scott so dear to men of experience are not absent even from 'The Bride of Lammer-

moor.'   There is matter in the book which belongs
evidently to the province of prose, as distinguished from that of the poetical imagination, an
excessive insistence on the work-a-day humour of
Caleb Balderstone, and quite sufficient insistence
on the prose delights of the conversations, how
admirable in themselves! between Bucklaw and
his swaggering henchman.   Poetical as the book
is, and dependent on this quality for its effect,
it hardly ever ventures into regions of such
height that matters more appertaining to prose
are altogether forgotten.   To see this, one does
not need to place it beside purely poetical compositions such as ' Hamlet ;' it is enough to place
it beside works produced in the same medium,
such as ' The Scarlet Letter,' since whatever be
the respective merits of the two romances, it will
not be disputed that Hawthorne's is the more
consistently poetical and touches less often on
the ordinary world.   'The Bride of Lammermoor' is a work differing in degree rather than
in kind from many of Scott's other novels, few
of which do not contain situations of which a
dramatist would have eagerly caught hold.
Nevertheless it differs greatly in degree; for
while in all the others it is the prose author who

especially arrests attention, this particular book
lays claim to be judged as a prose composition
with a poetical excellence, as a production in
which we have to do with a poet. Its place
among the Waverley Novels is singular. One
wonders how it happened that in this one romance
that side of Scott's genius which is elsewhere
subordinate, should have been exercised so freely.
It has been plausibly suggested that, the main
motif of his story leading him to think of 'Hamlet,'
he was insensibly drawn to model his incidents
on those in Shakespeare's tragedy, and that they,
thus formed, gave a colour unusual with him to
his thoughts. As Mr. Balsillie says in an admirable paper, unfortunately buried in the pages
of a defunct publication, 'The Ladder,' which
appeared in 1891—"A comparison of Scott's
tragedy of 'The Bride of Lammermoor' with
Shakespeare's 'Hamlet' will bring out several
points of curious interest," and he continues—
" The points of resemblance on the surface are
striking if they are coincidences merely." " In
each the hero's life is shadowed by an obligation
to avenge a father's wrongs. Ravenswood resembles Hamlet in not a few points. Both are
men of lofty aims, which are thwarted by their

terrible legacy of revenge. Lucy Ashton again is the twin sister of Ophelia, and falls under the same dark fate. Sir William is as astute a diplomatist as Polonius, and not quite such a caricature"—not at all a caricature, I should say. " If a ghost roused Hamlet to his duty, the spirit of blind Alice at the Mermaiden's Fountain reminded Ravenswood of his. The very grave-diggers of Shakespeare have their representatives in Scott's tale. The presence of Ravenswood at Lucy's funeral, and the stern challenge given and accepted there, remind one of the scene between Hamlet and Laertes beside Ophelia's grave; and if Ravenswood did not fall by the sword of Lucy's brother, he was on the way to do so, when, in fulfilment of the Wizard's prophecy, he found a tomb in the Kelpie's flow." But those incidents, while exhausting the list with which those of 'Hamlet' may be directly compared, do not exhaust the list of poetical incidents in ' The Bride of Lammermoor.' Ravenswood and Lucy never appear unless in some effective situation, set with dramatic propriety. Lucy and the Lord Keeper visit old Alice, a situation in which an Elizabethan dramatist would have delighted. On their return, Ravenswood appears

in the nick of time to save them from the attack
of a wild bull, and later on in the romance they
are detained by a storm in the ruinous castle of
Wolf s Crag. All these and many other incidents
are not only poetical in themselves, but are
treated far more poetically than is usual with
Scott. He appears to have set himself to write
a Shakespearian tragedy in narrative form, and
though possessing neither Shakespeare's imagination nor his sense of proportion, he has succeeded
in producing a work of consummate excellence.
It is worth while to notice how he has produced
it, and what reliance he places on the art of the
drama.

From the dramatic excellence of the book
there is little that detracts. That Scott should
introduce, in the midst of his scenes of passion
and feeling, humorous or matter-of-fact interludes, cannot be said to detract from it. The
English dramatists are famous for their fondness
for this device, and to what varying use Shakespeare has put it may be seen in ' Hamlet ' and
' Macbeth.' However, on these interludes, un-
objectionable and often of the highest merit in
themselves, Scott lays unnecessary stress. The
single fault of ' The Bride of Lammermoor ' is

that we have too much of them. Caleb is both
too farcical and too important, he breaks the
thread of our thoughts, and becomes interesting
for himself; he is not like Shakespeare's porter,
a mere aid to the action.   It is difficult to keep
the exact proportion in these things.   Hawthorne's 'Scarlet Letter' wants something of
that of which 'The Bride of Lammermoor' has
too much.   Hawthorne wants to have his feet
more firmly planted on the ground, Scott wants
to get rather more free from it.   He wants it
doubtless everywhere ; all his novels would be
improved and would gain in weight and depth
were he more detached from the realm of plain
affairs.   Even 'The Bride of Lammermoor'
would gain by it, and though in reality in 'The
Bride of Lammermoor' this attachment of his
is less obvious than elsewhere, in a sense it is
more obvious, just because in this romance he
has in general made a real attempt to leave the
work-a-day world behind.

Strange then is his success here, so strange
that with his especial devotees, with those who
love his flavour because it is his, 'The Bride of
Lammermoor' has never received quite the admiration it deserves.   If Scott had produced

O

works, which, considered singly, were, next to
Shakespeare's, the greatest works of the English
imagination, a feat which with all his excellences
he has undoubtedly not achieved, and if Scott
was pre-eminently a prose author, as undoubtedly
with all his poetical excellences he was, then the
works he produced while following his bent,
'The Antiquary' or 'The Heart of Midlothian'
or 'Rob Roy,' which rest on the merit of their
characters, are likely to be found most excellent.
If, in short, as an artist he had nothing to learn,
then the productions which came from him most
naturally, and in which he was not attempting
to get away from himself, must stand higher than
a book so conscious an effort throughout as
'The Bride of Lammermoor.' And much may
be said for this contention even if we put forward
no such claim for Scott as an artist. Still the
facts are to be considered. 'The Antiquary'
can have cost its author little trouble. 'The
Bride of Lammermoor' must have cost him much,
yet the 'Antiquary' is not a more striking success
in the domain of prose than the 'Bride of Lammermoor' in that of the poetical imagination.
All that can be said is, that when Scott was
writing as the nature of the novel led him, it

was easy for him to do wonders, but that when it came to adventuring into a new field he had need of his powers.

It is another question whether the story would not have gained if cast in dramatic form. One must admit, I think, that though the highest dramatic success is likely to be found in the drama, and not in an art which imitates it, the same artist who is able to make his narrative dramatic may be at a loss when he abandons narrative altogether. In Scott's case we have reason for congratulation that abstract considerations did not weigh with him. His work in poetry had given no indication that he was fitted even when at his best to write a great drama, and though he continued fitfully to write verses for some considerable time after 'The Bride of Lammermoor' was published, his poetical powers, ever since the production of 'The Lady of the Lake,' had suffered a decline. His power as a prose writer was at its height; in the medium of prose narrative he had already won by far the most substantial of his successes.

Fielding has been called the prose Homer of human nature; it would be as proper to call Scott the prose Shakespeare of human nature, for what

prevents him from being comparable with Shakespeare is just that—he is a prose Shakespeare—
and what makes him in a sense comparable with
Shakespeare is this, that for an essentially prose
author, for one of his constitution, and for one
working in his medium the sum of his achievement is not far short of being as wonderful.
Scott, need it be said, is never so profound, has
never so comprehensive a view as Shakespeare,
and thus the distance between Falstaff and
Hamlet is incomparably greater than that between Oldbuck and Ravenswood. For all that
there is the same sort of distinction. Falstaff
and Hamlet are conceptions at the opposite poles
of a poet's world, Oldbuck and Ravenswood at
those of the world, and wide and varied it is,
which is open to the novelist. Falstaff and
Hamlet are both poetical conceptions, but Falstaff comes near the world of prose, while though
Oldbuck is purely a prose conception, Ravenswood is one that intrudes upon the domain of
the great dramatic poets. Shakespeare is so
great a poet, that while remaining a poet he can
swoop down into a kind of sublimated world of
every day : Scott is so great a prose writer, that
while remaining a prose writer he can venture,

and venture with success, into the world of the
poets.   This is not the same thing indeed, for
the one world is far wider and more profound
than the other, but in its degree it is a comparable thing.

Let us turn for example to the scene at old
Alice's "winding." Ravenswood, startled by the
apparition of old Alice at the fountain, rides on
to her cottage, in front of which was the "turf-
seat placed under a weeping birch of unusual
magnitude and age," where in the opening of
the romance she had been found seated, as "Judah
is represented sitting under her palm-tree, with
an air at once of majesty and dejection." There
he finds the corpse awaiting the last offices
at the hands of three old crones, to whom he
gives directions respecting the charge of the
body. This duty performed he turns to remount
his horse.

"While busying himself," says Scott, "with adjusting
the girths of the saddle, he could not avoid hearing,
through the hedge of the little garden, a conversation
respecting himself, betwixt the lame woman and the
octogenarian sibyl. The pair had hobbled into the
garden to gather rosemary, southernwood, rue, and other
plants proper to be strewed upon the body, and burned
by way of fumigation in the chimney of the cottage.
The paralytic wretch, almost exhausted by the journey,

was left guard upon the corpse, lest witches or fiends might play their sport with it.

"The following low croaking dialogue was necessarily overheard by the Master of Ravenswood :—'That's a fresh and full-grown hemlock, Annie Winnie—mony a cummer lang syne wad hae sought nae better horse to flee over hill and how, through mist and moonlight, and light down in the King of France's cellar.'

"'Ay, cummer! but the very deil has turned as hard-hearted now as the Lord Keeper, and the grit folk that hae breasts like whinstane. They prick us and they pine us, and they pit us on the pinny-winkles for witches ; and, if I say my prayers backwards ten times ower, Satan will never gie me amends o' them.'

"'Did ye ever see the foul thief?' asked her neighbour.

"'Na!' replied the other spokeswoman ; 'but I trow I hae dreamed of him mony a time, and I think the day will come they will burn me for 't.—But ne'er mind, cummer! we hae this dollar of the Master's, and we'll send doun for bread and for yill, and tobacco, and a drap brandy to burn, and a wee pickle saft sugar—and be there deil, or nae deil, lass, we'll hae a merry night o't.'

"Here her leathern chops uttered a sort of cackling ghastly laugh, resembling, to a certain degree, the cry of the screech-owl.

"'He's a frank man, and a free-handed man, the Master,' said Annie Winnie, 'and a comely personage—broad in the shouthers, and narrow around the lungies—he wad mak a bonny corpse—I wad like to hae the streaking and winding o' him.'

"'It is written on his brow, Annie Winnie,' returned the octogenarian, her companion, 'that hand of woman, or of man either, will never straught him—dead-deal will never be laid on his back—make you your market of that, for I hae it frae a sure hand.'

"'Will it be his lot to die on the battle-ground then, Ailsie Gourlay?—Will he die by the sword or the ball, as his forbears hae dune before him, mony ane o' them?'

"'Ask nae mair questions about it—he'll no be graced sae far,' replied the sage.

"'I ken ye are wiser than ither folk, Ailsie Gourlay. But wha tell'd ye this?'

"'Fashna your thumb about that, Annie Winnie,' answered the sibyl—'I hae it frae a hand sure eneugh.'

"'But ye said ye never saw the foul thief,' reiterated her inquisitive companion.

"'I hae it frae as sure a hand,' said Ailsie, 'and frae them that spaed his fortune before the sark gaed ower his head.'

"'Hark!. I hear his horse's feet riding aff,' said the other; 'they dinna sound as if good luck was wi' them.'

"'Mak haste, sirs,' cried the paralytic hag from the cottage, 'and let us do what is needfu', and say what is fitting; for, if the dead corpse binna straughted, it will girn and thraw, and that will fear the best o' us.'"

These are not Shakespeare's witches. To transplant them to a prose narrative would be impossible, and, were it possible, when transplanted they would take no hold of our belief. Scott with his fine artistic sense—and how fine it was when he chose to give it play!—knew that had he introduced spirits of evil into his romance, he would have detracted from one of its chief merits, the firm grasp with which, poetical though it is, it keeps hold of the world of sense; and so

his old women, induced by their charnel-house
fancies to think themselves in touch with "the
powers of the air," are but old women still.
How much merit there is in this conception!
In poetry the creatures of the imagination have
an actual and visible life ; in prose, however vivid
are our fancies, we must know them to be such :
in poetry the imagination can create, but in prose
the belief in fable can do no more than influence
the character. Obedient to the limitations of
his art, Scott has done everything. Though he
has not trespassed beyond the province of fact,
he has succeeded in terrifying his readers, and
some of them, no doubt, even more than Shakespeare terrifies them, since there must always
be those who are more awake to material than
to spiritual alarms. The slow travelling mind
which refuses artistic credence to the weird
sisters, cannot but be struck by these gruesome
figures of Scott's, that show themselves una-
bashed in the daylight.

If we are ever to get an adequate conception
of 'The Bride of Lammermoor' we must judge
of it as a whole. Of all Scott's novels it is the
most artistic, and the best fitted to be so judged.
It stands out from the rest of them, not so

sharply, but much in the same way as 'Esmond' from the other productions of Thackeray. In most of the Waverley Novels, excellent though the story may be, we forget the story and remember the characters; in 'The Bride of Lammermoor,' excellent though the characters are, we forget the characters in our interest in their fate. The story proceeds for a time at leisure, till everything is put in order for the suddenly descending catastrophe, as Lachesis may turn the wheel slowly till Atropos cuts the thread; and though this swiftness of conclusion is an excellence that belongs rather to the drama than to the novel, 'The Bride of Lammermoor' is throughout so essentially dramatic that that is a merit in it which in 'Old Mortality' was a blemish. The romance follows roughly the lines of dramatic division. In the first act, an account having been given of the hero and heroine, their meeting is effected. The second and third acts are occupied with the various incidents marking the growth of their acquaintance, the third ending with the parting of the lovers. The fourth is devoted chiefly to the development of the counter-plot, which during the second and third has risen into prominence, and the fifth act, as in 'Hamlet,' narrates the hero's return and the subsequent catastrophe. Except when dealing with Bucklaw or with Craigengelt, the narrative has a dramatic swiftness; a few touches and Lady Ashton, Colonel Ashton, and Lucy's brother Henry take their places as effective subsidiary characters. Even Lucy, though she appears often, makes her effect quickly when she does appear. Ravenswood and the Lord Keeper are sketched with greater attention to detail, yet both always appear in character. Both comport themselves with the same kind of dramatic consistency as Balfour of Burley in 'Old Mortality'; neither varies as Oldbuck in 'The Antiquary' varies, · with the small but surprising variations of a slowly developing nature. They are figures seen with the insight of the poet, and, curiously enough, considered for his separate interest, Ravenswood is as good, as forcible, and as life-like as the more strictly prose figures that are so common in Scott's other novels: nay, what is more remarkable, since the wonder excited by Scott's achievement would be less had he abandoned the prose field altogether, Ravenswood is as good as the prose figures in 'The Bride of Lammermoor,' he does not suffer when placed

by the side of Caleb Balderstone, poetry does
not become theatrical by juxtaposition with
prose. On the contrary it is prose that suffers,
and Caleb, who is not intrinsically as much of a
caricature as Andrew Fairservice, seems, of the
two, the more overdrawn, because he is placed
in the more impressive surroundings.

, Nothing is more puzzling to the critic of
Scott than the combination in his nature of
extraordinary artistic insight, and an almost
constitutional levity in regard to his art. The
conception of Caleb Balderstone is an unusually
fine one. It is ironical, this idea of a retainer
with his mind set on dishes while his master is
thinking of death, and as Scott occasionally
manages it, it is irony of a very beautiful and
lucid kind. Moreover it was a *tour de force* for
him in his delineation of his serving-man to
pitch humour and pathos both so high, and yet
leave behind an ultimate impression of reality.
Admirable use is made of the conception of
Caleb, but at the same time a too frequent use.
The same note is struck too often and too
loudly. We see things as they are. The theft
of the supper, and the unending preparations,
become burlesque; the fictitious burning of

Wolf's Crag is too broad a stroke—Shakespeare's gravediggers might as well have played
at bowls with the skulls they disinterred—not
that Scott will allow even an occurrence so
much beneath the dignity of his sombre tragedy
to escape him, without showing to what account,
had he chosen to treat it seriously, he might
have turned it.

" Ravenswood," runs the narrative, " no sooner found
himself alone, than, impelled by a thousand feelings, he
left the apartment, the house, and the village, and hastily
retraced his steps to the brow of the hill, which rose
betwixt the village, and screened it from the tower, in
order to view the final fall of the house of his fathers.
Some idle boys from the hamlet had taken the same
direction out of curiosity, having first witnessed the arrival
of the coach-and-six and its attendants. As they ran one
by one past the Master, calling to each other to 'come
and see the auld tower blaw up in the lift like the peelings
of an ·ingan,' he could not but feel himself moved with
indignation. 'And these are the sons of my father's
vassals,' he said—'of men bound, both by law and gratitude,
to follow our steps through battle, and fire, and flood;
and now the destruction of their liege-lord's house is but
a holiday's sight to them !'
" These exasperating reflections were partly expressed
in the acrimony with which he exclaimed, on feeling
himself pulled by the cloak,—'What do you want, you
dog?'
" 'I am a dog, and an auld dog too,' answered Caleb,
for it was he who had taken the freedom, 'and I am like

to get a dog's wages—but it does not signification a pinch
of sneeshing, for I am ower auld a dog to learn new
tricks, or to follow a new master.'"

It is impossible to improve such passages, and
equally impossible to avoid wishing that they
had been set in surroundings less grotesque.
In the same way, the meeting between the
Marquis of A. and Lady Ashton in the hall of
the Lord Keeper's house, is both artistic and
impressive, but one finds oneself laughing as
one recollects that their carriages were near
coming into farcical collision at the entrance
to the avenue.

There are faults, perhaps, which the writer
could not readily avoid. It is no such easy
thing to turn a drama into narrative form, without either becoming tedious, or seeking the
relief which inconsequential humour affords, the
more especially if the author's genius inclines
him to excursions of the kind. What is noticeable is that here Scott should on the whole have
kept so free from them, the book being remarkable among his many remarkable productions,
not only for itself but as coming from him. For
while in the 'Bride of Lammermoor' there is
much that is characteristic of Scott, there is also

much of which before he had given only vague
forewarnings, a consistently dramatic intention, a
passionate intensity, and a poetical seriousness,
contriving in combination to challenge comparison with the work, not so much of his
successors in prose, as of his forerunners in
poetry.

In his historical novels it was a task of a
totally different order which he essayed, and it
would be a superficial criticism which neglected
the distinction. In the 'Bride of Lammermoor'
the action interests, as far as it is ever possible
for action to do so, for itself; in 'Quentin
Durward' it subserves as definite a purpose as
in 'The Antiquary.' In the latter, Scott's gaze
is concentrated on the characters, in the former
on the past age, which it was his desire to bring
back to us. In such novels as 'Quentin Durward,' 'Ivanhoe,' and 'Kenilworth,' the fictitious
story performs no other office than that of sus-
taining our interest; it is on what it lights up as
it shifts along that our real attention is fixed.
What reader of 'The Talisman' is the least concerned after the meeting between Richard and
Saladin, as to what happens to Sir Kenneth and
his fair lady? We must not look upon Scott's

historical novels as novels of action, though that
they are so there can be no question, any more
than we must consider them as historical narratives claiming to be judged by the ordinary
rules. They are in reality as much novels of
character as 'The Antiquary' or 'Guy Mannering,' the difference being this, that in his historical novels Scott is not studying the character
of individuals, but the character of a period or
reign. It is only when we so consider them
that the real weight of his achievement becomes
apparent, as also the futility of the objections
which are ordinarily urged against him as a
historical artist. We provide ourselves with a
complete justification for his playful dealing
with fact, without forfeiting our right to rely
on the more ordinary and extremely sensible
defence which has become stereotyped.

"A mixture of a lie," said the wisest of Lord
Chancellors, "doth ever add pleasure," and
one is reminded of the saying as one turns the
pages of the numberless essays, that find in the
Waverley Novels every literary virtue but the
virtue of historical exactitude. Scott gives us,
their writers complain, too bright a picture of
past times, the sun shines upon too many lords

and ladies, and even the serving-man and serf
have their little portion of pleasure, whereas do
we not know that for every lord there were a
thousand serfs, for every lady a thousand bond-
women, and that these unfortunates lived upon
black bread and water, and spent their time,
when they were not shrinking under the lash, in
forced and hereditary service? Do we not know
that the men who laboured on their lords' plant-
ations were consumed with an inward rage
against the distinctions between villeinage and˙
the tenures of free socage and knight-service,
and the whole lawyer and priest-supported
machinery for the oppression of the poor?
Have we not reason to suppose, exclaim these
writers, that the world of the Middle Ages was
for the majority a singularly unhappy one? what
judgment would we pass on a novelist who
wrote of the Roman Empire without taking
note of the harsh condition of the slave?

To misrepresent the attitude of these critics
is far from my intention, and indeed it is only
one of the questions here put into their mouths
that is not sure of an affirmative reply. The
world of the Middle Ages, the world in which
Richard jousted and Louis XI mumbled over

his beads, contained, doubtless, all the suffering
and all the inequalities which modern humanity
finds there: serfs were ill-treated, women were
abused and on the question of property there was
no sufficiently broad distinction between children
and cattle. Nor is it to be imagined that these
hardships passed unheeded; it does not require
a peculiarly sensitive organization to feel hunger
and the whip; here and there at the foot of the
social ladder it is certain that there were even
those who actively rebelled against their condition. Only here and there, however, for though
it may seem a paradox, it is probably true, that
those inequalities and hardships were less offen-
sive then than now. They were taken much
more as a matter of course, and since mankind
in the rough has always been inclined to believe
that whatever is, is right, and the fool, however
miserable his mental or physical state, to sing,
few thought of criticizing them. To view ancient
society as Mark Twain views it in his sincere
and interesting book, 'A Yankee at the Court
of King Arthur,' is to lose the historical per-
spective. Those features of the life of the feudal
ages, which to a modern American are especially
noteworthy, passed in the days of long ago with

P

what appears to us now as incredibly little
notice. Mark Twain himself acknowledges as
much when he emphasizes the difficulties which
his astute piece of modernity experienced in
making clear to the bondsmen the hardness of
their lot. Had Scott painted the Middle Ages
as a modern historian would paint them, neglecting nothing of their sordid detail, he would have
sacrificed not only half the effect, but half the
truth of his picture. We should have learned
what the Middle Ages were, and not, what in
a measure we have, how they appeared to the
men of the Middle Ages. It is this, then, that
on the question of Scott's essential accuracy, we
have to bear in mind. We have to remember
that, however much more patent than Scott has
represented them, were, the uneven chances of
life in the particular state of society which then
existed, the attention of the poorer classes would
not be directed solely to this, but also and surely
in a greater degree to the same picturesque and
outstanding incidents which catch our attention.
Let any one suppose, what requires no exertion
of fancy, that a serf had seen in one day another
serf flogged, and "the pleasant and joyous"
passage of arms at Ashby-de-la-Zouche, and then

let him ask himself of which of these occurrences the serf, stretched at night on his straw
pallet, would be likely to dream—let him ask
himself that, before he dismisses the Waverley
Novels offhand as historical caricatures. As
much as this may be urged, before reliance is
placed on the truth which Bacon's aphorism
crystallizes, in general denial of a charge that
has been too frequently and lightly brought.

But the fact is that no novelist, no literary ›
artist, is bound, in dealing with a historical ˄
period, to satisfy the same minute standards by ˛
which a historian is tried. He is bound, when ˄
treating of a historical period, unless writing,
as Shakespeare in 'Lear,' without a historical
intention, to remain true to the character of the ˄
times of which he speaks, but he is not bound ˟
to do more than this. As long as he represents ˒
his antique world much as in general outline it ˅
was, he is free to pay tribute to his art, and to ˒
exalt to an undue pre-eminence the more striking ˒
characteristics of the society he depicts. Richard, ˒
perhaps, was not altogether so chivalrous as
Scott represents him, nor James so petty, nor
Elizabeth so masculine; but something must be
allowed to the claims of the picturesque, some-

thing must be forgiven to the artist if his imaginations become at times "imaginations as one would." "Doth any man doubt," asks Bacon, "that if there were taken out of men's minds vain opinions, flattering hopes, false valuations, imaginations as one would, and the like, but it would leave the lives of a number of men poor shrunken things?" And certainly without Scott's historical romances we, as regards our conceptions of the periods he has made real to us, would, to some extent, be shrunken. The freedom he took was no unreasonable freedom, being, if the worst were allowed, but "the mixture of a lie." Nor can it be said that any one is likely to suffer from Scott's habit of exalting the knightly characteristics of "the knightly days of old." "It is not," says Bacon, "the lie that passeth through the mind, but the lie that sinketh in and settleth in it that does the hurt," and Scott's lie does not sink or settle in. Those who depend on a historical novelist for their knowledge of history can hardly be numerous, and cannot be wise. It would be to inquire too curiously to ask how far in the Waverley Novels we receive an exact account of the periods described.

All that can be expected of a literary artist,
and possibly all that is to be desired, since
where precise accuracy is unobtainable it is best
not to attempt it, is that he should give us a
rough sketch of the character of the epoch.
The historian comes to Scott's historical novels
biassed against them; he knows well that the
method of the great romancer is not the method
of the careful recorder, so far indeed from it
that it almost looks as if he had had a standing
quarrel with fact.   To turn to many of these
historical romances is to find the dates carelessly, I had almost said carefully, distorted.   To
take two instances from a hundred.   Leicester's
first wife, Amy Robsart, had been dead for
fifteen years before he entertained Elizabeth at
Kenilworth, yet in the novel Amy Robsart
meets the Queen in Leicester's gardens during
the famous *fêtes*.   Shakespeare did not begin
writing plays, on the earliest computation,
before 1589, yet Elizabeth in 1575 is represented as quoting from 'Troilus and Cressida,'
which must thus have been the production of
a boy of eleven.   The novels are full of such
instances, and the historian who finds a novelist
indulging in licence of this kind may be excused

if he looks with suspicion on his general estimate of a historical period. Nevertheless to
understand the service Scott did for history, we
must keep clear in our minds the distinction
between misrepresenting the facts, and misrepresenting the character, of a reign. His in-
accuracy in the one case is no more remarkable
than his essential accuracy in the other. He
cared nothing for the letter, so long as he was
true to the spirit; nay, so right is his instinct
for the spirit of the times he describes, that the
facts twist and turn themselves anyhow till they
come to fit. In an account of Elizabeth's reign
it was necessary that Shakespeare should figure,
so Shakespeare finds himself born thirty years
before his birth. Despite their thousand in-
accuracies, their carelessly arranged dates, their
jumble of fictitious fact and fiction, 'Ivanhoe,'
'Kenilworth,' 'The Fortunes of Nigel,' 'Quentin
Durward,' and 'The Abbot' carry us back not
to the past only, but to definite periods of the
past. The world of 'Kenilworth' is as distinct
from the world of 'Quentin Durward,' as the
world of 'Quentin Durward' is distinct from
that of 'Ivanhoe.' In each of them we catch
the air of the time; we get, so to speak, its

feeling right, we appreciate its character.   And
looking for no more than this, we may reasonably refuse to range ourselves with those who
exclaim against works which, properly understood, perform their office so well.

Regarded from this attitude ' Ivanhoe,' the most
famous of those historical novels, is also one of the
most instructive.   We read the account of Cœur
de Lion's actions in the pages of many historians,
and if the chronicler is dry it seems dull, if
the chronicler is vivid, improbable.   But Scott,
though he uses unnecessarily improbable incidents, makes Richard at once a possible and an
interesting figure.   There are no inequalities in
the portrait.   Free from any bondage to fact,
and having caught the salient features of
Richard's nature, he proceeds to emphasize
them.   There is no question of any action
being out of Richard's ordinary course, being
in need of explanation, or putting the rest of
his doings into the shade.   Everything seems to
be in place because everything is in character,
and Pelion placed beside Ossa does not look as
huge as a smaller solitary hill.   Largely by the
frank use of this method, the whole of that old
world, which as we read the history books

appeared so dim or so fantastic, is quickened ·to
an extraordinary life.   Robin Hood steps out
of the coloured illustrations to the children's
stories and moves about with the zest of the
old ballads that had made him their hero: the
Crusaders wear their armour not like actors at
a masquerade, but as men to the habit born:
the pageantry of the reign dances before us—
proud maidens of high Saxon degree, pretty per-
secuted Jewesses, grand-masters, jesters, swine-
herds, and disinherited sons.

'Ivanhoe' has been called the best of historical
novels, and though, since it wants the necessary
sobriety, it is hardly that, one sees why it should
have caught public attention more than 'Quentin
Durward' and 'Kenilworth,' novels with greater
historical merit, and a firmer grasp of life.   The
public, in passing its bizarre judgment, has
appreciated rightly the difficulty of the three
achievements.   Hard as it was to represent the
courts of Louis or Elizabeth, it was incomparably harder to represent the clanking soldiers
in 'Ivanhoe.'   Armour is now but "monumental
mockery," and let the links in the chain-mail
coat be ever so real, Harry Percy is but a
pasteboard figure on the stage.   The world of

tourneys, of lady-loves, and by my halidoms,
has gone down the wind.   Poetry alone can
revivify the age of steel.   Something of her fire
and elemental ardour is needed to sustain these
chivalric passages that seem to us, living in an
age of sobriety and prose, a little too ardent, a
little boyish.   The strange oaths remind us of
a time when we were deeply impressed by the
mere quantity of them, the battle-axes that
split so many crowns have a smack of the
curiosity shop, and we are amazed when we
remember that men once went out to decide
a quarrel without the danger of being blown by
an unseen enemy into a million smithereens.
What a pother, we repeat to ourselves, about
the rusty gate of the castle of Torquilstone,
when one of the dynamitards of modern fiction
had but to take a packet from his waistcoat-
pocket and puff the " fortress of no great size "
to the four corners of the " casing air."

Do what we will, we cannot take it seriously,
and those who account ' Rebecca and Rowena '
the best of parodies have to remember that
seldom a better subject came to a parodist's
hand.   The period in which ' Quentin Durward
is cast is nearly two hundred years nearer our

own day than that of 'Ivanhoe'; the action of
'Kenilworth' takes place quite at the end of the
days of chivalry. While 'Quentin Durward' is a
novel dealing chiefly with the council-chamber,
and 'Kenilworth' one that does not introduce
warfare, 'Ivanhoe' is a romance of the field. As
the world grows older, we add little to our
knowledge of love-making or statecraft, but
fighting changes with the weapons employed.
Milton's aërial battle between the spirits of the
nether and those of the upper air, would be an
odd incident for a novel, and though Crusaders
have a better right to a prose existence than
fallen angels, they are not comfortable material
for a novelist.

Difficulties enough then faced Scott when he
set about the composition of 'Ivanhoe.' In such
circumstances, most men of fifty, one imagines,
would have made an exceptional effort to get
in touch with possible fact, and if they had had
to deal with warfare, abductions, and torture-
chambers, would have made as light of them as
possible; would, for instance, have diminished
the personal prowess of their heroes, and the
magniloquence of their abductors, and decently
hurried over those passages in which they

meddled with hot iron. Another and less
obvious method approved itself to a teller of
tales as experienced as Scott. Far from shirk-
ing the natural difficulties of his subject, he
invents minor incidents essentially boyish, and
lingers over them with boyish delight. Richard,
as we know him in history, too heroic a figure
for prose fiction of an ordinary kind, appears in
'Ivanhoe' in as thunder-smiting a mood as that
of Geraint, when in the 'Mabinogion' Enid drives
before him the horses of twelve slaughtered
knights: Front-de-Bœuf hurtles through the
pages of the romance as magniloquence per-
sonified, and his creator catches the infection.

"'Seize him and strip him, slaves,' said the knight, 'and
let the fathers of his race assist him if they can.'
"The assistants, taking their directions more from the
Baron's eye and his hand than his tongue, once more
stepped forward, laid hands on the unfortunate Isaac,
plucked him up from the ground, and, holding him between
them, waited the hard-hearted Baron's farther signal.
The unhappy Jew eyed their countenances and that of
Front-de-Bœuf, in hope of discovering some symptoms
of relenting; but that of the Baron exhibited the same
cold, half-sullen, half-sarcastic smile which had been the
prelude to his cruelty; and the savage eyes of the Saracens,
rolling gloomily under their dark brows, acquiring a yet
more sinister expression by the whiteness of the circle
which surrounds the pupil, evinced rather the secret

pleasure which they expected from the approaching scene, than any reluctance to be its directors or agents. The Jew then looked at the glowing furnace, over which he was presently to be stretched, and seeing no chance of his tormentors relenting, his resolution gave way."

'Ivanhoe' is full of such strained situations. If Rebecca is to have an interview with the Templar, she must have it on the dizzy edge of the battlements ; if Robin Hood is to shoot, he must shoot better than William Tell ; if Front-de-Bœuf's castle is to be burned, it must be burnt by the demented Ulrica ; and if all is to end happily, the happy ending must be brought about by the mock funeral of Athelstane. But all this only goes to show with what zest Scott threw himself into his task, how anxious he was to bring everything into line, and how little deterred by any fears of improbability. A tale about the Crusades appear improbable! he would have said to the literary aspirant, only take care you make it improbable enough. And so he carries it off, begging the reader to excuse him for adding a little artistic heightening to events that might otherwise appear too matter-of-fact. He has no doubts himself, and, as we read on, compels us to feel ashamed of our incredulity, for after all if half-a-dozen of the incidents

could have happened so could all the rest. Who
ever doubted the word of Scheherazade?

There are not many passages in 'Ivanhoe'
that would seem natural if transferred to any of
the more sedate of the Waverley Novels, yet
there is one portion of the book which does not
depend for its effect upon the genial exaggeration of the whole, that part, I mean, which deals
with Rebecca and Rowena. The contrast
between the two women is both striking and
natural, and though they sometimes appear in
forced situations, they are both drawn with a
regard for a different kind of truth, from that
which Scott had in his mind when he flung off
his lively sketches of Richard and his Crusaders.
It was a fortunate thought that induced him to
contrast with his proud Saxon maid, his proud
Jewess, since both in a sense are outcasts, though
their circumstances have a different complexion.
The position of Rowena, the daughter of a race
though conquered, royal, ministers to her pride ;
Rebecca remains proud despite her position.
The claims of the one, though considered
fantastic, were respected by the Normans, as
even in France to-day the most convinced
republican pays some deference to the descend-

ants of the old *noblesse*, but the other could advance no claims that, proceeding from a Jewish usurer's child, would meet with anything but contempt. Rowena's pride consequently is always in evidence, and only put by when her heart is touched; Rebecca's can hardly have been suspected, and appears only at the important moments of her life. In their final meeting the contrast is brought out with great delicacy. The fault of both characters is that they are laboured. Even Rebecca, on whose creation Scott had excuse for priding himself, moves through his pages with a grand tragedy air that is not quite the manner of life. They are interesting chiefly as affording an example at once of his excellence and weakness as a painter of women. His attitude towards both is similar, with the delineation of both he took pains, and yet while the one is a portrait of great merit, the other comes near being a lay figure. To understand how it so happened, is to understand two things about Scott, which, as distinctive of a master of the novelist's art, are well worth notice : his high sense of the bearing of action upon character, and his consistent practice, whatever the liberties he allowed himself in dealing with

events, of putting into his novels people corresponding with those whom he saw.

That Scott was deficient in his knowledge of
female character has been too often admitted
by his sturdiest admirers as a kind of propitiatory
sacrifice to those who cannot see, as they do, in
each successive Waverley Novel a masterpiece
of art ; even Mr. Hutton, one of the safest and
most discriminating of his critics, is betrayed into
saying, "Except Jeanie Deans and Madge Wildfire and perhaps Lucy Ashton, Scott's women
are apt to be uninteresting, either pink and white
toys, or hardish women of the world," and though
the sentence is immediately after so qualified as
to retain little value as a presentment of fact, it
remains as a kind of gathering up of the general
censure expressed.   It may be doubted whether
even as a censure it will not admit of being
reduced, and whether Mr. Hutton is not prevented by what in Scott he terms natural chivalry
from taking account of all that can be pleaded
in justification.

To deal with the question generally, it will be
granted at once, as indeed Mr. Hutton proceeds
to grant, that the portraits of women of the
peasant class in the Waverley Novels, of women

with a definite occupation, and who have the same or nearly the same chances of developing character as men in a corresponding rank in society, are unusually interesting. The waiting-women of Scotch nationality,—for an instance we may take Jenny Dennison in 'Old Mortality,'— are painted, if with a little exaggeration, only with the exaggeration of truth, and to many critics it will appear that the delineator of Edie Ochiltree is to be seen in the delineator of Meg Dodds. Equally good are the female "characters,"[1] to use the word in its Scotch sense, the women, whatever their situation in life, like Mause, Meg Merrilees, and Lady Margaret Bellenden, who occur in such various guises and so often. All this and more Mr. Hutton grants, when he introduces still another exception in favour of some historical figures. But even among the ladies of middle rank there are some that cannot be cursorily dismissed, and there must be those who, while admitting that Scott's

---

[1] "Men or women with some accentuated trait or traits of character, oddity of personal appearance, or style of talk, marking them off from the common herd of human kind, are those who are usually known as 'characters,'"— 'Reminiscences of Innerleithen and Traquair,' by Thomas Dobson.

method is not Thackeray's, find Diana Vernon quite as live a creature of fancy as the Amelia Sedley who so little repays analysis, Catherine Seyton as she whisks a vanishing skirt into the old house in the High Street something other than a pink and white toy, and Clara Mowbray, with her affected gaiety and mind perplexed, by no means a hardish woman of the world.

However, it can be no part of the duty of sane criticism to deny that Scott has in his extended gallery several portraits of ladies who are pink and white toys. Miss Wardour and Julia Mannering are two indisputable examples, if indeed Miss Wardour is not also one of a hardish woman of the world. Rose Bradwardine and Lucy Bertram have a good deal that is pink and white about them, and even Edith Bellenden might be so described by unkindly critics. There are others of course, but taking the five only as examples it will be noticed that the more interesting are those who are brought most in touch with events. Lucy Bertram, because she has more to disturb her, is more interesting than Julia Mannering, and so is Edith, since she finds herself placed in a situation of unusual interest. And this it is, I think, that will supply Scott's

Q

justification. Character in the world in which we live is not only best displayed in action, but is often wholly dependent upon it for its development, and consequently it commonly happens that people who have nothing to do with action have very little character at all. In the periods of which Scott wrote, the number of Julia Mannerings and Miss Wardours must have been far from inconsiderable. To a " home-keeping " girl, to a woman living a guarded life, and hedged about from all the roughness of circumstance, the world must have been too colourless then, to provoke much response. Even to-day, when the opportunities of education are as open to one sex as to the other, that one can meet with Miss Mannerings, just as one can meet with young Lovels or Waverleys, is a fact too notorious for denial. The question is how far an artist is bound, if he deals with such "homekeeping" people, to make them interesting, to make more of them than Scott has troubled to make. Undoubtedly Miss Austen's Emma Woodhouse is interesting, and yet when the last page is turned her mind and soul are still negligible quantities. But how far is an artist bound to follow this method, nay, how far is it possible for one who deals with great actions to do so? May it not be said that for a success of this kind there is necessary a pre-Raphaelite attention to detail, a concentration of interest on one point which is inconsistent with the artistic dictum that a picture must be seen as a whole? A painter who paints a wide expanse of mountain country must miss the petals of the flowers that dot his foreground, just as a painter who gazes at the petals will miss the outline of the hill. Emma is what she is, because Miss Austen looks at her through her hands, but Scott, whose view is on a wide field, sees Julia Mannering in her corner.

Nor is Thackeray's practice, when carefully considered, however different in manner from Scott's, inconsistent with this view of the limitations which on one hand or the other attach to the literary artist. Amelia, a passive figure, is made interesting, but it is at the expense of an amount of detail which to those unaccustomed to Thackeray's leisurely habit becomes tiresome. There are even critics to whom Laura and Mrs. Pendennis, women of no great attainments, but who contrive, without taking any considerable share in the plot, to capture our affections, seem dull. With all his power of analysis, Thackeray's female characters who possess the most general attraction, Blanche, Becky, and Beatrix, are intertwined with whatever action there is in the novels where they occur. And even if the exception which Laura and Mrs. Pendennis constitute, be fully granted, the comparison is unfair. 'Pendennis' is a novel of still life in a sense in which none of Scott's novels are. Throughout almost the whole of them, irrespective of whether the interest of character or action predominates, there goes a breezy air of movement, a kind of flapping briskness that suggests a boat putting out to sea. If the world to which Scott introduces us is ample, there is also a noble amplitude in his manner, an amplitude that contains a hint, as far as it was possible for a prose artist to give it, of Shakespeare's own.

We have to turn to Shakespeare to learn how far it is possible for an artist whose world is even wider and more full of movement than Scott's, to make a female character interesting without the help of action or the encumbrance of undue detail. The heroines of the tragedies,[1]

---

[1] Hermione and Hero may for the present be classed with the heroines of the tragedies, since they too, though occurring in comedies, are connected with a great action.

since necessarily connected with a great action,
as also the merely farcical characters, since Scott's
success with them is undisputed, may be put
aside.   And if we confine our attention to the
comedies, and think of the ladies who there
have interested us most, the names that come to
the tip of the tongue are those of Portia,
Rosalind, and Beatrice, all, it will be recognized,
deriving a great part of their interest from the
unusual situation in which they come to be
placed.   Portia and Rosalind go masquerading,
and Beatrice is most herself when she befriends
her cousin in the chapel.   Throughout the
comedies the general rule will be found good ;
almost all the ladies who especially interest us
assume the habit or go through the experiences
of men.   Sylvia it is true does not, but Sylvia is
a pink and white toy, and so indeed is Bianca :
Celia and Nerissa do not, but neither is a centre
of attraction : the ladies in ' Love's Labour's
Lost ' are but shadows, Olivia fades before Viola,
and " sweet Anne Page " is a name.   Perdita and
Miranda are the only instances to the contrary
that occur to the mind, and of these it is sufficient
to remark that they are essentially poetical
conceptions, perhaps the two most poetical

conceptions of " the supreme poetical power in
our literature." It would be a preposterous
demand to make of a novelist that he should
attempt to rival such achievements, that wherever
he has a Miss Wardour he should give us a
Miranda, that he should do often in prose what
Shakespeare at the top of his poetical genius does
seldom.   Shakespeare attempts it seldom, since
qualities such as Miranda possesses—obedience
perfect yet in no sense the offspring of a cowed
individuality,sweet yet non-insistent dignity,sym-
pathy all embracing, tenderness playful and con-
summately feminine—are best displayed and best
understood in action, Desdemona being nothing
else than a Miranda with a superb occasion.

The point to notice is not that Shakespeare
has once or twice triumphed over difficulties
quite too hard for Scott, but that he, too, where
he has not action to help him, "has his pink
and white toys."   The difference is this, that in
Shakespeare we do not notice their existence,
since, they not being playthings for a poet, he
has consistently neglected them or relegated
them to the second place. The Anne Hathaways
of the world, he would wish to tell us, with that
light optimism which was so often his, do never

really marry the heroes, their business being but to
dance at the weddings of the Rosalinds or Portias
for whom poets pine. I confess that to me it
seems that Scott in this matter has been more
true at least to the truth of prose than Shakespeare has been. Looking out over the society
about him, he found among his Dianas and Lucy
Ashtons, and among the Perditas whom he
could not paint, many a Miss Wardour and
Miss Mannering, and these colourless characters
by no means always to be neglected or playing
second fiddle in the odd concert of human kind.
To study them in detail was no part of his
business, to have done so would have been to
have interfered with his large plan of getting a
world between the covers of a book, while to
ignore them was for him as impossible as any
other deviation from his constant habit of recording what he saw. Those who wish poetical
truth, and it is of the higher service, may turn to
Shakespeare, but those who wish to learn the
plain matter of fact—not as to how the world
goes, for Scott is often unreliable there, but about
the people who compose it—will turn to the
Waverley Novels. Where an author is salutary
he is not always palatable.

CHAPTER IV

MISS AUSTEN

A MARSH dotted here and there with a deluding oasis, in which one stumbles, till a side step, taken perhaps from a lack of caution, perhaps by unavoidable chance, finally misleads, and one sinks, a bubble or two bearing witness to this sudden addition to the bog :—a road baked by a pitiless sun, up and down which dust-clouds are blown, obscuring the outline of a city too distant to convince the traveller that what he sees thus casually is not the product of fancy, part of the phantasmagoria of dreams :—a sea, subject to episodical storms across which, and beneath a sky often of a heavenly clearness, a small ship struggles pertinaciously to a port attainable by the master mariners :—these are conceptions easily distinguished, but the world takes shape according to the colour of the glass

through which we view it, and as our glass may
have a thousand colours, so a thousand simili-
tudes are necessary to represent its varying
appearance. Between most of them there is this
resemblance, that few are lightly favourable, for
look past the world as men may, who is unaware
of its blackness, or blind to its difficulty? " I
have been studying," says Shakespeare's Richard,
" how I may compare

" This prison, where I live, unto the world."

How admirably, exclaim the theologians,
the place where human business is conducted
puts the passions and emotions to the proof!
and since it is from them if from any one that
we should get a picture of rose, we shall not
find elsewhere pronouncements more flattering.
There is something at the back of the gayest
appearing optimism which disguise does not hide.
At bottom, our reflections on our position have a
grave turn. We conceive the world as a marsh or
a tumbling sea, rather than as a meadow, or a
pool breaking on some occasion into trivial
waves. Life, we are not in the habit of thinking
of as a luxurious transportation from point to

point, or such a journey as a young lady will
readily describe.

There have been women—it is written in the
literary history of various countries—who have
dealt successfully with life at large, but these are
they who in their devotion to their story, their
drama, or their novel have put aside conventional
restrictions, and bid the standards of young
ladyhood defiance. They are women who wish
to be judged as authors, who ask of the
public that it should neglect the sex of a serious
writer, as readily as it neglects the age; they are
not Miss Austens. Miss Austen—and it is at
once her greatest limitation and her peculiar
charm—said nothing that a lady might not say
in a drawing-room, and spoke only of those
matters which may be supposed to be dearer to
women than to authoresses. Every one has heard
the story of Congreve, who, when Voltaire came
to see him, hoped that he might be visited as a
gentleman rather than as a literary man, and
every one has delighted in Voltaire's retort that
one need not leave one's country to meet people
with good manners. The excuse for Congreve's
foppery is that the cant of authorship is disagree-
able, and that a man of the world may reasonably

desire to be distinguished from those who are
always either talking about their literary productions or priding themselves upon them.
That portion of pardon which is granted to an
author will be readily extended to an authoress.
When Madame de Stael expressed a wish to
meet the author of 'Pride and Prejudice,' Miss
Austen characteristically replied that she would
go nowhere under that title where she was not
received as Jane Austen.   It is difficult not to
sympathize with her exaggerated sensibility.   A
male pedant is often tiresome, but a female
pedant is often ridiculous, and about Miss Austen,
who has moved so many to laughter, there was
never anything ridiculous.

Still, a lady who writes books in this spirit
runs the danger of not appreciating the seriousness of her business, a lady who considers herself
as by nature a member of a protected class, and
by accident or whim, an authoress, is not likely
to sacrifice any conventions to her art.   A young
lady who persists in writing about the world as
a young lady should, forces us back upon the
question—how is a young lady to describe it?
The truth is that the position of woman in letters
is one of some difficulty.   She is confronted on

the one hand with the custom that prescribes for the conversation of women an artificially selected range of subjects, and on the other with the custom of the great artists, prescribing an altogether different selection. If she writes as custom prescribes she will not speak of things of which the great artists are in the habit of speaking. If she writes as a great artist might, she will speak of many matters which are not discussed in drawing-rooms.

It was the fortune of Miss Austen, surely a genius of an altogether exceptional kind, who had no idea of writing anything which any one would be surprised to discover had been written by the daughter of a clergyman, not only to avoid artistic failure, but to achieve a highly remarkable artistic success, by a prompt recognition of the conditions under which she wrote. Many women there have been as anxious about the proprieties as ever she was, who have amused their leisure, or earned their bread by a swift succession of artistic failures : women who, though precluded by the fastidiousness of their temperaments, or the nicety of their circumstances, from speaking adequately of great subjects, have constantly attempted them. To men-

tion instances would be invidious, but every one
has read novels written by women, fitted to shine,
but not in literature, and dealing with the most
tremendous matters, with the same primness one
would expect in a nursery tale. Miss Austen,
appreciating the conditions in which she was
placed, and giving the rein to her impulse, fell
into no such error. Not only does she not speak
of the world, she makes no pretence of speaking
of it. She knew her province, and in her
province she achieved, at least so we must think
till another Miss Austen gives us evidence to
the contrary, all that was humanly possible.

Her life is a short story. She was the daughter
of George Austen, a handsome and scholarly,
but in no way exceptionally distinguished clergyman, who in those days of happy pluralists, had
almost as of course, his two livings, his horses, his
relations better off in the world's goods, and his
circle of friends, some of the middle, some of
the upper class, but all equally welcome at his
Horatian rectory, where indigence and luxury
were equally unknown. Her mother was Cassandra Leigh, a lady of the same position as her
father, trained to the same habits of thought, and
coming from a family with good sense and good

brains.   Miss Austen was the youngest of seven
children, five boys, and two girls.   Of the boys,
the eldest became an occasional writer, the
second was adopted by a wealthy relative, the
third became a clergyman, and the fourth and
fifth, entering the Navy, reached the degree of
Admiral.   Her sister Cassandra, her senior by
three years, became her devoted confidante.
"Cassandra's," says Mr. Goldwin Smith, "was the
calmer disposition with less seriousness; Cassandra, it used to be said in the family, had the
merit of having her temper always under command; but Jane had the happiness of possessing
a temper that never required to be commanded."
Born on December 16, 1775, Miss Austen
spent the first twenty-five years of her life at
Steventon.   Thence, her father growing old, and
resigning the cares of his office to his son, she
proceeded to Bath, where the family remained till
some little time after his death.   Her mother
with her two daughters then took up her residence at Southampton, from which place the
three removed in 1809 to a cottage offered them
by the brother who had been adopted by their
relative, and in proximity to his place at Chawton
near Winchester.   In this cottage the mother,

now old, and the two attendant daughters remained for the rest of Miss Austen's active life.
In 1817 she was transported to lodgings in Winchester for the sake of constant medical advice.
She had been ill for some time, and did not long
survive her change of residence.   Towards the
end of July in that year her family followed her
body to the grave.

For all practical purposes the periods spent at
Bath and Southampton were unproductive.   At
Steventon, in the last five years, three novels
were written, and at Chawton in five years,
three more.   For ten years Miss Austen observed
quietly, for ten years she wrote quietly and
deliberately, and, during the forty-two years of
existence which she obtained, nothing, as far
as we know, happened to her which was not
decorous and quiet.   Her life passed in a
round of simple duties and enjoyments.   For
her neighbours as well as for herself there was
a plethora of fireside delights and homely
aspirations.   Born and bred among people
of the literary middle class, all interested in
believing the habits to which they conformed,
the moral rules they obeyed, the religion they
professed, to be by some stroke of patriotic

fate the best possible, and all, as a matter of fact, without hesitation believing this, she was surrounded by an atmosphere, if not of reasoned, at least of secure doctrine. It was a secure England on which the news of the French Revolution burst, and it took some time to rob it of its security. Always open to the influence of convention, the professional classes were not likely to be the first to break away. Undistinguished and yet not unknown, their members have everything to lose by challenging the general opinion. They have not the " coign of vantage " of a public character, or the plain obscurity of a mechanic; in custom they are rooted, custom provides for them, and why should they quarrel with societies where they find their comfortable niche? Add to this that Miss Austen was not the friend of Erskine or the acquaintance of Mackintosh, but the demure daughter of a country vicar, and we get a notion of the ideas with which she would come in contact. I suppose there seldom existed a more conventional society than that which was to be found in the vicarages of England about the beginning of this century. The influences which surround an Established Church are continually making for lethargy, and a hundred years ago they had uninterrupted sway. The Pope had long ceased to be a present fear, and the preacher who had thundered on the terrors of the Papacy would have thundered to nodding benches. The first fury of the Revolution had spent itself, and even had it not, the feast of Reason had never been set out before the doors of a Hampshire parsonage. "If Dr. Grant feared anything," says Mr. Goldwin Smith, summing up the matter in a sentence, "it was that the green goose would fail to appear on table after evening service, not that the Goddess of Reason would be enthroned on his communion-table, or eject him from his living." The Oxford movement emphasizing the claims of Catholics; the progress of the critical spirit, the fruit of Protestant inquiry, with the consequent lightening of a load of encumbering tradition; all this, with its wide effect on the Church, lay hid in the unimagined future. Constitutionally lethargic, the English rural clergy preached drowsily to drowsy hearers from the text "Whatever is, is right."

Their daughters, for in those days the duti-

R

fulness of daughters was an accepted fact, presumed not to contradict them. Some, such as Miss Austen, must have known, but would perhaps have been shocked to hear, as they certainly would not have said, that virtue consisted not in obedience to any formulae, but in an inclination of the mind, and that every civilization with its set course for propriety is but the arrangement that seems best at the time. Others, and they were the great majority, had not arrived at this conception. The reader of Erskine's speeches is struck with the few occasions on which that admirable advocate bases his argument on the true ground for tolerance, the fallibility of opinion, an idea existing in the highly conventional society he addressed, that to say openly that anything was a convention was as much as to say that it was bad. "Angels and ministers of grace" defended the social philosophy of Lord Eldon; Church, King, Lords and Commons, marriage and property, these were institutions as they existed, to wish any of which "mended or ended" was a mark of impiety. To dispute with orthodoxy about religion was, to borrow the simile of Dr. Johnson, like putting a pistol at a man's head, as

if any one had a vested interest in a serious
opinion, as if it were not the business of
every one, by taking thought, to arrive as near
as for him is possible at the truth of the
discussion.

It is true that we have not yet any reason
to plume ourselves on our attitude towards open
inquiry. About everything considered essential
the mass of the public in 1897 believes itself to
be as indisputably right as Miss Austen's public
believed· itself in her time. The work of the
independent thinker, where his powerlessness
does not protect him, has always been done
amid the babel of awakened prejudice: Dr.
Pangloss is a phenomenon by no means extinct,
and it is only in 'Candide' that he has not a
temper. For all that, to-day another attitude
is in the air. We have moved so fast of late
that it is difficult to believe there is any finality
in our present ideas, or that we shall not need
to borrow from the future and the past to
correct them. Everywhere there are men, and
those not merely among the educated few, who
have come to realize that it is necessary to
listen, and that while something may be gained
by argument, nothing can be done by quiescence.

We appear to be approaching that far-off epoch, how far off those best acquainted with the social history of the last thirty years and its pitiless acrimonies may form some conception, when heat in the conduct of any serious discussion will seem as impertinent as it does now in the field of scientific inquiry. Certain it is, that if we ever reach it,—and millenniums do not hurry, —we shall have reached a society in temperament the antithesis of that in which Miss Austen lived, when the ability or worth of a citizen was measured by the amount of approval granted to his opinions. Opinions then were luxuries to be looked on with suspicion. What need had any one for them, when there was a multitude sufficiently acquainted with the truth about everything? This guardianship of the majority extended itself to trifles. If a youth saw no harm in Sunday travelling, he might miss the hand of Anne Elliot. If Miss Crawford smiled at country parsons she offended her suitor. If any one chose to be a Radical, he was promptly visited with the penalty of exclusion from the delightful pages of Miss Austen.

This was the atmosphere in which she grew up, an atmosphere moreover which there is no

reason to suppose was uncongenial to her.
This was the society in which she lived
perfectly happily, and against which, there is
abundant evidence in any one of her books, she
never for a moment rebelled. To have, as she
phrased it, good principles, to accept the views
of other people, to drink tea, and to talk a deal
of harmless gossip, this was the sum and end
of human perfection. To marry, well, if possible,—that is, if consistent with love,—but in
any case to marry, this was the sum and "end of
every man's desire." An authoress with such
a gospel, or an authoress at heart entirely
heedless of any other gospel than this, will
assuredly not go a great length. An adequate
conception of human society which, like a poplar
tree, in the bulk remains stable while the separate
leaves are in a state of unending agitation, she
cannot have. The relation of the individual to
that congeries of individuals which we call the
world, and the resultant comedy, the vagaries of
never-dying passion, the alternations of desire,
and the general movement of ambitious dust, of
this she can have no appreciation. "A mad
world, my masters," says Shakespeare, as he
opens his volume of plays; "a various world,"

says Scott, as he invites us to the large feast
he has prepared. But how was Miss Austen to
depict it ? The people among whom she moved
were far from various or mad, on the contrary,
they were monotonously sane; their sanity was
surprising. The great world—the world in
which Byron, Goethe, Napoleon moved—lay
beyond her little circle; to speak of it adequately she would have had to travel far from
her friends, far from home; to enter into its
meaning she would have had to do violence to
herself. Milton, said Dr. Johnson, was a genius
that could cut a Colossus from a rock, but could
not carve heads upon cherry-stones, a remark,
the sense of which we are better able to
appreciate when detached from its amazing
context; but however untrue of Milton with the
application to his sonnets which Johnson intended, it is a saying that needs only to be
reversed to be true of Miss Austen. She
indeed was a genius that could carve heads
upon cherry-stones, but was constitutionally
incapable of cutting a Colossus from a rock—
and to know this was her signal felicity. Only
once in the concluding chapters of 'Mansfield
Park,' does she trespass into a domain too

high for her, and there the trespass is but slight.

Such an account of an authoress may not appear appetizing, but in those things we are apt to judge theoretically from too high a theoretical standpoint. Few of us take the trouble to chronicle the foibles of our neighbours, but as a matter of fact each of us derives much amusement from observing them. If we can imagine that by some magical process all our sensations and thoughts, evoked during a round of visits, dances, and dinners, were put down on paper, we can also imagine, I presume, that their perusal would be of interest. They interested us at the time, why should they not afterwards interest others? How much more interesting the record of the thoughts of a woman with extraordinary insight into the niceties of character, and with a charming, and even unique power of gently satirical comment! If this were all Miss Austen's novels were, they would still be read by maids. But Miss Austen in her novels, in those sparkling commentaries on a dull society, has done ever so much more than the mere chronicling of her impressions. In the first place she presents us with a story, which though in her later novels a little long-winded, is always of sufficient interest to keep the attention.   In the second place she arranges her *dramatis personae* with an unerring eye for effect, contrasting for instance Mr. Bennet with his wife, or Fanny Price with Mary Crawford. In the third place she draws largely on a fertile and always credible invention, and is constantly elevating a nonentity into an individual by the use of the nicest shades of caricature. In a word, she had, if we make allowance for her limited scope, every art of the novelist. To a great action alone she was indifferent. It is amazing to see how carefully she hurries over those passages which, in the course of her story, bring her near emotion and passion. In 'Sense and Sensibility,' where such an opportunity came nearly to her hand, she deliberately avoids it. The trivialities of daily life press forward, Willoughby's story is thrown into the background, and only narrated when it has become a piece of past history. "The passions are perfectly unknown to her," says Miss Brontë, " she rejects even a speaking acquaintance with that stormy sisterhood."   It is so obvious that one is apt to forget its importance.   An

authoress who does not touch these matters
of which the great masters speak, cannot be
ranked with them. A novelist of character
who dispenses altogether with great action,
with every action that is not trivial, can tell us
little of weight about character. The best
conjurers bring on the stage a whole world of
accessories. Miss Austen takes a sheet of
paper and quickly folds it into the likeness of
a hundred things. To delight an audience with
the manipulations of the paper modeller needs,
no doubt, an unexampled deftness of hand, but
to perform the Indian basket trick one wants
also a boy and a basket.

To describe the delicate art of Miss Austen,
" metaphor," says Mr. Goldwin Smith, "has been
exhausted ; " in minuteness of treatment she has
been compared to the Dutch painters, in fineness
of colour to the artist on ivory. Yet her work
resembles that of the Dutch school of painting
in nothing except its minuteness, her humour is
not jovial, and the manners she describes seldom
coarse. Like the miniaturist, her space is limited,
but unlike the miniaturist, her method is not
cramped by the smallness of the space. It was
but a small part of life she saw, but she saw it

whole. Her figures are as large as life, but in life they are not large. From day to day she sat in her parlour, taking note of everything that passed; watching, at first with saucy delight, and also with occasional sensibility; watching, in her later days with an added tenderness, but also with an added propriety, and perhaps just a touch of bitterness, the trivial panorama that unwound before her. With an authoress of Miss Austen's stamp criticism is soon exhausted. Her works, unlike those of authors of wider range, give no opening for the eccentricities of private judgment, and such distinctions as exist among them are of necessity fine. The likeness between 'Sense and Sensibility' and 'Mansfield Park' is far more obvious than the difference, and there is an appearance of freak in laying emphasis on what needs to be suggested to be seen. Yet to grasp the distinction and to see in what it consists is to get a clearer idea of Miss Austen's general capacity, as it is also to appreciate in detail to what kind of excellence a writer with her interests is limited, and by what means she may please.

At Steventon three books were written—'Pride and Prejudice,' 'Sense and Sensibility,' and

'Northanger Abbey;' ten years later, at Chawton, three more—'Mansfield Park,' 'Emma,' and
'Persuasion.' It will be convenient to glance at
them in their order, though the order itself is a
little confused. The first step towards the composition of any of Miss Austen's masterpieces
was taken with a rough sketch of 'Sense and
Sensibility.' Thereafter she struck off the first
sketch of 'Pride and Prejudice,' revised 'Sense
and Sensibility,' and then wrote 'Northanger
Abbey,' which was also the first of the three
to leave her hand. This was in 1803, but
'Sense and Sensibility' and 'Pride and Prejudice' did not receive their final touches till
about ten years later. 'Northanger Abbey'
may thus be taken as showing most clearly the
traces of 'prentice work, 'Sense and Sensibility'
and 'Pride and Prejudice' as together the fine
flower of the first period. Viewed in this light
'Northanger Abbey' acquires a new interest, for
though speaking literally it was not a precocious
production, Miss Austen, in 1803, being twenty-
eight, there is reason to suppose that no altera-
tions more than verbal were made on the copy
completed five years before. The actual plot,
we know, was concocted later than those of the

other two books of this period; but in them even
the incidents may, as the years passed, have
been subjected to some slight change.   It is a
matter of little consequence, as the plot of 'Northanger Abbey' is of little account.   Intended
partly as a skit on Mrs. Radcliffe's romances, the
book is furnished with a story intentionally
weak.   What is of importance is the treatment,
and here we are on safe ground in concluding
that Miss Austen, in her first production, had
not quite found her manner.   The book is short,
and yet it is not innocent of tedium.   Its great
success, a patient study of a girl with a colourless character, though a triumph of miniature art,
does not catch the fancy.   In the centre of a
novel one looks for life, nor is there enough in
the other characters to give to the book a lively
air.   Whatever action there is, is devoted to the
elucidation of the character of the heroine; such
other personages as occur are, contrary to Miss
Austen's later habit, character-sketches.   We
have to take them as they first appear, with the
consequence that they are either faint or a trifle
over-coloured, wanting perhaps that vivacity
which is essential even to the lightest caricatures.
Miss Tilney is a shadow, and Mrs. Allen might

have been made more of. General Tilney is a
character whom it is not easy to understand; if
he is meant as a Radcliffian parody, the parody
is not incisive; if he is meant as an actual person,
he is but a half-hearted performer in the part
of heavy father. Henry Tilney, his son, who
talks at large, and is intended to be clever and
serious and good, conveys the impression of
being a little conceited, and something of a prig.
The comic personages are undeniably amusing,
but their attitude is fixed. Young Thorpe provokes laughter, not altogether without arousing
the suspicion that he is there to be laughed at.
Isabella, his sister, a more active figure, comes
nearer, though even she misses complete success.
Throughout the book Miss Austen gives the
impression of hesitating between two attitudes,
and while in the end she generally maintains
that divided one which was to become habitual,
it is not clear whether her real intention was to
be gayer or less gay than she appears. Parts of
' Northanger Abbey' are quite solemn, there
being no obvious call for solemnity, parts are
written in a spirit of laughter, which does not
somehow impress one as hearty, while here and
there is a tendency to sententiousness. When

Henry Tilney cannot conveniently be utilized as
an organ for the delivery of stock reflections,
Miss Austen comes in her proper person to his
aid. If we compare the novel with 'Pride and
Prejudice' we see that what its authoress wanted
was a more lively interest in her characters, and
what she had to fear was the approach of seriousness: if we compare 'Pride and Prejudice'
with it we see how soon she learnt to make her
slight plots interesting by the enthusiasm with
which she told her story, and to carry off any
tendency to seriousness by the sparkling movements of her wit. 'Northanger Abbey,' like
everything else Miss Austen wrote, has a charm
of its own; its especial interest for the critic is
due to its showing traces of the same manner
which reappears in her later works. Her detail,
for instance, she takes quite seriously, "painting
her rose" with the same touch of almost laugh-
able gravity which is observable in 'Mansfield
Park.' In 'Pride and Prejudice' she is herself
amused as the record of trivialities runs from
her pen.

Than this last surely never was there a book
written which has given more harmless pleasure
to those who have come under its spell. As we

open its pages, we bid adieu to a world of sordid
cares and troublesome interests, and though we
do not wander into fairy-land, for Miss Austen's
world is always matter-of-fact, we do catch a
breath of an air less severe than that which we
habitually draw, and find, if not fairy-land, at
least a touch of the lightness of fairy-land brought
down to us. Everything, strictly speaking, is a
little out of life. Mrs. Bennet is a little too
silly, Mr. Bennet a little too clever, the abduction a little too gay, Mary a little too funny, and
Darcy too like the Prince of Dignity Castle.
But while everything is heightened, nothing is
heightened overmuch : the play of fancy, the
constant and nimble satire, lend a light not its
own to the humdrum society described. Still,
the society is there, the picture is as accurate as
could be drawn by a woman full of girlish freshness and mature wisdom suddenly turned arch.
Indeed it is difficult to know what to praise
most in this delightful book, its essential truth,
or that touch which takes clean away from it
anything of the sordidness inseparable from the
plain presentation of fact. Here are all those
people : the foolish, scheming mother, the witty
and not unselfish father ; the girls, sensible,

beautiful, giddy; the bucks so preposterously dandified; the inanely pompous vicar, the bowing mayor—just as they lived, and yet not just such: speaking, let us say, in their natural voices, dressed in their usual clothes, but moving to a music a little brisker than any to which in their real lives they had made pretence of keeping time.

How is this miracle in miniature effected? By no breach of the laws which govern the artistic world. There is as much activity in 'Pride and Prejudice' as there is in 'Ivanhoe.' The incidents are small, but they are constant, and each does its office. We look through the kinetoscope, and we see the maiden dancing as featly as those whose weight is something in stones. A breeze ruffles a pond, and the toy-boats are driven out to sea, or to harbour, buffeted as unceremoniously as a ship on the Atlantic. There was not an infinite deal to be shown,— the delectable folly of a mother of five; it was enough that Mr. Collins should propose or Lydia be married,—the reproving wit of a man who has every excuse for being as witty as Miss Austen can make him; it was sufficient that in his household he should have had to reckon a

silly wife and three silly daughters,—the nature
of an English girl, sensible, artless, debonnaire;
all that was wanted was a country town, a
dearly-loved confidante, a dance, a sister's chill,
a visit from the Blankshire regiment, a lover
with supercilious airs, a chance meeting at Pem-
berley. Elizabeth Bennet tripping about her
mother's white painted rooms is as real as Diana
Vernon on the heath. With her, sunning in Miss
Austen's humour, where is the reader who has not
fallen in love? and though her heart does not
beat sufficiently strongly to leave an ineffaceable
impression on ours, we have only to renew our
acquaintance to feel the old attraction. Lord
Beaconsfield professed to have read 'Pride and
Prejudice' seventeen times. One wonders no
longer that a statesman who was so often in
such company should have found himself on the
side of the angels. This is the triumph which
Miss Austen is always bringing off, and she
brings it off because though her range is limited
she is mistress of her range. Let the events be
as unimportant, or even as in her later books as
occasional as possible, not one is wasted. She
has her eye always on her characters: Lady
Middleton has a spoilt child; how would Lucy

Steele behave to it ?   Darcy writes a neat hand;
what would Miss Bingley say?   Willie Price is
in want of pocket-money; what "considerable
sum" would represent the beneficence of Mrs.
Norris?   These are the questions that interest
her.   A straw will show which way the wind
blows if one holds it up to learn about the
wind.   Only on some days, and on them Miss
Austen keeps indoors, the wind is so strong that
the ground is clean swept of straws, and if one
found one twirling in a corner, it would be
snapped away before one could hold it up.   She
is the perfect master in little; in her own domain
she has always the knowledge and resource of
which Scott is so often heedless: the moment
she steps out of it he leaves her standing.

'Sense and Sensibility,' a work of the same
period, and subjected to the same process of
revision as 'Pride and Prejudice,' is very similar
in tone.   Of the two novels it has been generally
considered the inferior, perhaps because there is
no Mr. Bennet or Mr. Collins, perhaps because
there is Edward Ferrars, perhaps because Willoughby's record is darker than is wanted for
drawing-room comedy, and his confession too
noisy for a drawing-room.   It is plain that the

contrasts are sharper, and the shades of character-
drawing not so fine as in 'Pride and Prejudice,'
Elinor being possibly too sensible, Marianne too
much the food of enthusiasm, and Mrs. Jennings
too boisterously amusing. Nevertheless 'Sense
and Sensibility' comes in a good second to Miss
Austen's masterpiece, and some, their judgments
notwithstanding, it will charm as much. Of the
two productions it is, on the whole, the younger ;
it wears more openly the "exulting outside look
of youth," and had Miss Austen never depicted
the character of Marianne her picture of English
girlhood would have been too consistently sensible. Every woman is not as sane as Elinor, as
judicious as Elizabeth, as proper as Fanny, as
teachable as Emma. On the contrary, there are
women, and those to be met with on other than
rare occasions, whose passionate desires swamp
their reason, who decide not by the head but by
the heart, women who act as Marianne Dashwood acts, with the same generous candour, and
the same confiding enthusiasm.

"At that moment," says Miss Austen, when Marianne
recognizes in the ball-room the lover who had deserted
her, "she first perceived him; and her whole countenance
glowing with sudden delight, she would have moved

towards him instantly, had not her sister caught hold of
her.

"'Good heavens !' she exclaimed, 'he is there,—he is
there !—oh, why does he not look at me? Why cannot I
speak to him?'

"'Pray, pray be composed,' cried Elinor, 'and do not
betray what you feel to everybody present. Perhaps he
has not observed you yet.'

"This, however, was more than she could believe herself; and to be composed at such a moment was not only
beyond the reach of Marianne, it was beyond her wish.
She sat in an agony of impatience which affected every
feature.

"At last he turned round again and regarded them
both ; she started up, and pronouncing his name in a
tone of affection, held out her hand to him. He approached; and addressing himself rather to Elinor than
Marianne, as if wishing to avoid her eye, and determined
not to observe her attitude, inquired, in a hurried manner,
after Mrs. Dashwood, and asked how long they had been
in town. Elinor was robbed of all presence of mind by
such an address, and was unable to say a word. But
the feelings of her sister were instantly expressed. Her
face was crimsoned over, and she exclaimed, in a voice
of the greatest emotion, 'Good God, Willoughby, what is
the meaning of this? Have you not received my letters?
Will you not shake hands with me?'"

One seems here to catch a faint echo of
those women who, springing from the pages of
Bandello and Boccaccio, took form on the
Elizabethan stage, that romantic feminine growth
of Italy which is often found transplanted and

flowering in another clime. That Marianne's
sensibility is exaggerated has been said often
and with justice, but the effect of exaggeration
is produced, not by the situation itself, which is
only graver and not less natural than others in
the novel, but by the length and monotony of
its treatment. The distress of the character has
always the same cause, and is always in evidence,
whereas an artist who had had an instinct for
serious action would have given some new turn
to the events, and thus avoided the artificial
effect of repetition. Miss Austen, whose art has
been compared to photography, has some of the
limitations of the photographer. A photograph
of one mood is as true as the photograph of
another, but a photograph of strong emotion
will fail by its fixity to convey the impression of
truth.

Another and infinitely different woman in
'Sense and Sensibility' will serve as an illustration of this. Like Marianne she appears
always in character, but she never wearies.
With a broadly comic figure there is not the
same necessity to vary the mood. Laughter is
effortless, and a reader will laugh three times
over three different presentations of the same

"humour," where he will not sigh twice over the same heroics. Literary analysis is not always justified of its labour, and possibly literary analysis will not help us to decide why it is Mrs. Jennings obtains a firmer hold of our affections than any other of the female butts of Miss Austen's wit. It cannot be her rather senseless interest in matchmaking, for Mrs. Bennet is as a matchmaker quite as inveterate, and if it is her goodness of heart, why is it that Miss Bates does not elicit kinder feelings? It is less of a sacrifice to confer benefits on a bevy of beautiful young ladies than to tend the last helpless days of blind and stupid age. It may be that Mrs. Jennings' promiscuous benevolence does happen, in a degree unusual for promiscuous benevolence, to be of service to those whom she comes across. Her meddling does no harm, she is always in high spirits, in an exuberance of wealthy good-humour; we are sorry for "poor Miss Bates," but Mrs. Jennings' loud laugh is extremely infectious. Mr. and Mrs. Palmer, who dance attendance on her, have the same kind of merit in miniature. They are out of nature, of course, but then it is not likely that they were intended to be otherwise. They come in just at those places where the narrative begins to drag, and the introduction of a couple of drolls is welcomed as a relief.

"'You and I, Sir John,' said Mrs. Jennings," addressing her host across the dinner-table, "'should not stand upon such ceremony.'

"'Then you would be very ill-bred,' cried Mr. Palmer.

"'My love, you contradict everybody,'" said his wife, Mrs. Jennings' daughter, with her usual laugh, "'do you know that you are quite rude?'

"'I did not know I contradicted anybody in calling your mother ill-bred——'"

A novelist must be full of vivacity before she condescends to farce so broad, but then 'Sense and Sensibility' and 'Pride and Prejudice' are the gay offsprings of youth.

Very different is the tone of 'Mansfield Park,' justly considered its author's most finished production. But in reading we are conscious that half our wonder is gone. The result may be, and in some ways is, more considerable than anything achieved by the earlier efforts. In 'Mansfield Park,' Miss Austen's art is seen in its most delicate form, her style is quieter, the effects she produces with it are even subtler than before. Nevertheless it is the mature fruit of a mature tree. What delights incomparably in

the books of the first period, is the union of
girlish freshness, of youthful zest, with the
admirable mental balance which only experience can give. "Is it possible," asks Mr.
Jowett in his diary, "for youth to have the
experience and observation and moderation of
age, or for age to retain the force of youth?"
Miss Austen's powers grew and deepened, but
in her first books we find the sense and discrimination of her last, and it is this which taken
together with their gaiety gives to them their
peculiar charm.   It is as if it were possible to
be at once old and young, as if a girl were to go
to a ball, dance it out, and enjoy everything as
much as any one there, with the full unreflecting
reception essential for perfect enjoyment, and
yet immediately after see the matter with the
eyes of one who had gone to judge of the
characters.   This union of youth and age then,
of things hardly ever found together, gives a
mark even more distinguishing than excellence
to such a novel as 'Pride and Prejudice.' 'Mansfield Park' is altogether an old book, perfect
perhaps if we leave out of account the melodrama of the conclusion, and the occasional
flapping of an extremely white white choker, but

still old, with all its merit with none of the
merit of youth.

'Pride and Prejudice' is gay, 'Mansfield Park'
is almost sombre; in 'Pride and Prejudice' the
minute touches are dashed in with laughing
haste; in 'Mansfield Park' everything is laboriously minute; in 'Pride and Prejudice' there
is a smile for every one, and every one deserves
a smile; in 'Mansfield Park' Mrs. Norris is a
character altogether repulsive, on whom sympathy
would be wasted. A real figure enough this
petty tyrant of a paltry sphere, but from 'Pride
and Prejudice' one would not have learnt that
Miss Austen had her acquaintance, or that of
the set which surrounds her. Sir Thomas
Bertram is of a genus extinct, Lady Bertram
the most indolently selfish of stupid ladies, and
Edmund Bertram with his "principles," his
reputable and shallow judgments, the most exasperating of heroes, so exasperating that one
thinks not once of the old saying that in the
beginning there were three species, men, women,
and curates. From these one turns with relief
to find no relief in Julia and Maria, Thomas
Bertram, Yates, and the "lady-killer" Crawford.
But how delightedly one discovers among them

Mary Crawford and Fanny Price, the two most
delicately-drawn figures in the whole of Miss
Austen's delicate gallery. Nothing could be
happier than their juxtaposition—the friendless
Fanny doing in the plain innocence of her nature
the offices of an universal friendship, and Mary
fingering her harp in the seat of the parsonage
window and weaving the spells of beauty and
mirth. One is pleased too with the fitness of
things that arranges for Cinderella having enough
of the leaven of Cinderella in her to find in
Edmund the fairy prince, and provides for the
princess, a rather mundane one who thinks
much of her lover's chance of a baronetcy,
ultimately escaping him. One is pleased with
the *dénouement*, however little with the means
by which it is brought about. Mary's brother
and Bertram's sister, who is married to a certain
Mr. Rushworth, elope together, and the light
comments and practical suggestions of Mary
result in a final quarrel between her and her
fiancé. The reader familiar with Miss Austen's
earlier novels exclaims in mild astonishment
when he is brought up by an incident of this
texture, a violent departure from ordinary conduct, with neither passion nor seriousness to

explain it.   It is true that occurrences of this
kind have given opportunity not only to trage-
dians, but in 'Mansfield Park' the incident,
narrated with the precision of a newspaper,
brings us too near to the atmosphere of the
divorce court, and Miss Austen's treatment of
it to that of the Sunday-school.   There is no
serious medium, she would give us to understand,
between talking extravagantly of sin, and treating such matters as of little account.   "Let
other pens .dwell on guilt and misery," she concludes near the end of the book, "I quit such
odious subjects as soon as I can, impatient to
restore everybody, not greatly in fault themselves, to tolerable comfort, and to have done
with all the rest."   There must be a strange
comfort in Pharisaism, else sympathy with the
sect had not survived.

On the point of art it is clear that an action
the extreme opposite of magnificent, must, to
be justified, have an effect proportionate to its
importance on the characters of the chief actors
or spectators.   What the incident emphasizes
in 'Mansfield Park,'—that a woman so much of
the world as Mary, and a man with so little
knowledge of it as Edmund, were bound to drift

apart,—trifles had already shown. It was singular
that Miss Austen, so wont to rely on trifles,
should have concluded her tale in this fashion;
and in her next production, as if sensible that
she had dealt with matters unsuited to the
style with which she charmed, she turned to a
lighter theme. In 'Emma' there is nothing
more serious than a secret engagement, with
the consequence that we are once more free to
be innocently amused with her intimate knowledge of the intricacies of character and the
resources of a humorous situation. The book
is distinguished by the same excellences, if also
by the same defects, arising from limitation of
view, which were observable in former productions. Mr. Woodhouse, the comic male
figure, a perfectly true portrait, if we allow ever
so little for conscious and humorous exaggeration, reminds us of the work of her youth; Mr.
Knightley, with more than a suspicion of sententiousness, but with sense enough to carry it
off, of many of her heroes; and Mr. Elton of her
numerous farcical sketches. The mere story,
though less inclined to drag than that of 'Mansfield Park,' is not quite so interesting as usual,
but the mere story, again as usual, is of practi-

cally no consequence : every page is the result
of quiet observation, of acute study of the
motives which govern ordinary conduct. Miss
Bates, at first reading, and, till one knows the
plot, a little tedious, becomes better at every
perusal, and I think the passage of years may
be noted in the fact that in one of her last books
Miss Austen selects as her female butt a character whom we feel under some necessity to
pity. Her humour, which in ' Mansfield Park '
had given place to a more serious wit, breaks
out again everywhere. Less gay than in ' Pride
and Prejudice,' it is as irresistible and often
more mellow. We forgive Mr. Woodhouse for
his iterated reference to Perry, take Emma's
solitary sally on Miss Bates' loquacity quite .
seriously, and seriously wish it unsaid. There
can be no question of an artist's power to deceive
when one becomes scrupulous that an imaginary
old lady should not receive momentary offence.
But there never was any question as to the
actual life of the chief characters in this book.
Emma, who is said to be pretty, but who has
nothing else remarkable about her—and that is
not remarkable with Miss Austen's heroines—
who is not particularly clever, and who rarely

comes near emotion, not only interests but
charms. She is young, and has the charm of
youth; she is active, and has the charm of activity;
she is alive, and has the charm of life. It is
not quite certain indeed,—there must occasionally
be a doubt with an authoress occasionally so
impersonal,—whether Miss Austen, her ideas not
being ours, was as much affronted as her modern
readers at the essential littleness of Emma's
first appearance; but to entertain the suspicion
is the province of a grudging criticism, and
certainly there is not a line in the portrait which
does not add to its truth. To live in a villa,
with a nicely-ordered lawn in front of the parlour-
windows, and a dozen or so trees scattered over
the enclosed acre or two through which the
drive ceremoniously winds, and this villa playing
the part of manor-house for the neighbouring
village, must be a trial for any one. Emma
Woodhouse, by no manner of means a great
lady, unaccustomed to mingle in society where
great ladies find their like, meeting no one than
whom she was not taller by an inch, must necessarily have thought something of her position.
Outside the village she knew it was not great,
inside she felt it to be magnificent: what was

there to prevent her from feeling those influences
which tug at the hearts of those whom a great
and careless novelist has swept into the large
basket labelled " snobs "? But how pretty is her
gradual emancipation from the necessary result
of her surroundings, what a good wife she must
have made for Knightley, and how often her
glowing smile must have sealed the nascent
lecture within his lips! No doubt, like all Miss
Austen's later heroines, she would recognize,
when her fit of gaiety was over, how eminently
proper it was that her husband should have felt
the desire to reprove : no doubt in the solitude
of her chamber, she would amuse herself with
her prim little moralizings, and think over and
over again that " she had never been more
sensible of Mr. Knightley's high superiority of
character."

The truth is that the continued study of an
artificial and trivial society has its effect upon
the mind, and we must put up ungrudgingly, for
the flood of humorous and sage comment amid
which we find such flotsam and jetsam, with
those prim little moralizings of Miss Austen's
later years. The judgment of a writer whose
field of vision no large interests cross, is bound

to become stereotyped, and even in ' Persuasion,' the novel of the six which Miss Martineau put first, there is a number of little things we could do without, the unamusing folly of Sir Walter Elliot, the precisian tone with which the authoress views the selfishness of Elizabeth and the Sunday travelling of her cousin, and the queer indifference, impossible for a robust morality, with which Anne views the shifty dealing of Mrs. Smith. A nature strengthened by the contemplation of great events could hardly, one thinks, have expressed itself thus, and yet how much sweetness and breadth of view was necessary to tell in just Miss Austen's way the beautiful love story of Wentworth and Anne. We forget the primness of many of her reflections, as we listen to those sentences with which charm is inextricably blended, and which seem to speak of a longing on the part of their writer for a different air. We forget them, as we come across again and again such passages as this, bringing a light tenderness and a beautiful innocent gaiety among the streets and into the rooms where dust and habit settle.

" Prettier musings of high wrought love and eternal constancy could never have passed along the streets of

Bath, than Anne was sporting with from Camden Place to Westgate Buildings. It was almost enough to spread purification and perfume all the way."

Camden Place to Westgate Buildings, we repeat to ourselves, how frank the recognition of the plaster and lime amid which now-a-days Cupid has to discharge his shafts, how like a sparrow's pipe in a city setting off the absurdity of man's elaborate arrangements.

This is not the tone of 'Pride and Prejudice,' and perhaps it would not be too much to say, if weight were to be given to fine distinctions, that each of Miss Austen's novels has a flavour of its own. But to say so is only serviceable if we keep in mind their essential similarity. It is no part of praise to hide what every one, given an account of her method, would suspect, and what every one reading her novels must see. " It is marvellous," says Mr. Goldwin Smith, " that Jane Austen's range being so narrow she should have been able to produce such variety. But narrow we must remember her range was, and recurrences or partial recurrences of the same characters and incidents are the consequence. We cannot help seeing the likeness between Henry Tilney and Edmund Bertram, while Edward

T

Ferrars is a feeble germ of both. We have several pairs of sisters, and sisterly affection is a constant theme. There is a close resemblance between Wickham and Willoughby, and a considerable resemblance between both of them and Henry Crawford." The instances might be multiplied indefinitely. Much of the fun of 'Pride and Prejudice' depends on the vulgar matchmaking of Mrs. Bennet, much of the fun of 'Sense and Sensibility' on that of Mrs. Jennings. Marianne is in love with Willoughby, Emma fancies herself in love with Frank Churchill: both are carried off in the end by elderly suitors who have been on the stage for a considerable time. In 'Pride and Prejudice' the heroine is proposed to by the wrong man, a similar fate befalls the heroines of 'Emma' and 'Mansfield Park.' All in the end make brilliant matches. In 'Sense and Sensibility' Edward Ferrars believes Elinor to be in love with Colonel Barton, in 'Persuasion' Captain Wentworth believes Anne Elliot to be in love with her cousin. Edward is fortunately saved from an entanglement with Lucy Steele, Wentworth is saved equally fortunately from the consequence of an entanglement with Louisa Musgrove. In all the novels

there is a great house forming in some way,
whether for purposes of description or matchmaking, the centre of attraction,—in 'Pride and
Prejudice' Bingley's, in 'Sense and Sensibility'
Sir John Middleton's, in 'Northanger Abbey'
General Tilney's, in 'Mansfield Park' Sir
Thomas Bertram's, in 'Emma' Mr. Knightley's,
in 'Persuasion' the Musgroves'. Even where
there is the broadest distinction between the
characters, there is, as in the cases of Mr. Collins
and Mr. Elton, occasional similarity in their
treatment. Both are clergymen, both for different reasons are ridiculous, both make absurd
proposals, both are promptly rejected, both find
immediate solace in another quarter, and the
married life of both affords Miss Austen opportunity for some of her sagest satire.

All this not only may but must be admitted,
yet with all this there is a singular diversity, an
absence of exact repetition which is truly remarkable. The distinction is a shade, but the
shade is almost always there. Undeniable as is
the resemblance between Wickham, Willoughby,
and Henry Crawford, they are all distinct; Wickham has not the dash of Willoughby, he is a
fainter, less generous, and far more consistently

selfish character. Henry Crawford is both like
and unlike them, for Henry Crawford has brains.
"Henry Tilney," says Mr. Goldwin Smith,
criticizing Macaulay's criticism, " shines more in
small talk than Edmund Bertram, and his
figure catches some of the special liveliness
which pervades the travesty, but otherwise the
two characters might be transposed without
injury to either novel." It is folly to dogmatize
about imaginary characters, but there must be
some who will dissent from this judgment.
Catherine Morland would not have attracted
Bertram, and Henry Tilney would have
married Miss Crawford. Mrs. Bennet and Mrs.
Jennings are as broadly distinguished from each
other, as both from Miss Bates. Marianne's love
for Willoughby is different in kind from that of
Emma for young Churchill. Knightley and
Colonel Barton, the fortunate suitors, are not in
the least like. The men of fashion, Darcy,
Bingley, and Frank Churchill, are as different
from each other as men of fashion can be.
Edward Ferrars' entanglement with Lucy Steele
is not creditable. Wentworth's engagement to
Louisa Musgrove was a wholly innocent mistake. Elizabeth Bennet is no more like Mari-

anne, than Marianne is like Emma. Mary
Crawford, Fanny Price, Catherine Morland, and
Anne Elliot are all individuals. The incidents
rather than the characters are repeated, and they
are repeated with a difference. To a sight
sufficiently keen, even among summer flies there
are no "heads without name," and as one thinks
of the array of nicely distinguished figures, going
through the same unpretending round of
pleasures and anxieties, which Miss Austen has
scattered over her pages, one exclaims in astonishment—what diversity, what likeness, amid such
sameness how much variety! As one thinks of
them one can find it in one's heart to forgive
those critics who have not been able to refrain
from introducing the names of Shakespeare and
Scott. But in reality, and for any purpose of
service, no comparisons could be more misleading. Scott's world, being a world of prose, is
distinct from Shakespeare's world, emphatically
a world of poetry. But both have a world to
deal with, both are capable of creating, both are
continually creating people, who, if they were
vivified, would not have the least understanding
of each other. What does Meg Merrilees know
of Lucy Ashton, or Falstaff of Lear! In Miss

Austen's society all the members are on calling or bowing acquaintance. Anne Elliot would have found fault with Mrs. Bennet's manners, but she might easily have passed an hour in the same drawing-room. Had Elizabeth taken advantage of Mr. Bennet's remark—"If any young men come for Mary or Kitty, send them in, for I am quite at leisure,"—and dispatched Captain Wentworth to him, he could not have been dissatisfied. True, not Shakespeare himself could have done more with the society Miss Austen saw than she has done : her achievement, given her materials, is as remarkable as anything in the world. A daisy is as remarkable as a Victoria Regia, but to say so is not to institute a comparison. If critics learn, as there is danger of their learning, to speak of Shakespeare and Miss Austen, it will be odd if some one with a sense of proportion is not provoked to retort—Shakespeare and five-o'clock tea.

The marvel is that the place of a writer whose range and view were as limited, and whose philosophy was as plainly empirical as Miss Austen's, should be as undisputed as Shakespeare's. We pay to her as ungrudgingly the respect which is her due. While Shakespeare thunders and

lightens to our continual amazement, and Scott
surprises admiration with his mass of generous
work, Miss Austen insinuates herself into our
affections.   Picking her way delicately, she
moves at her best with the gayest heart.
Whether she is depicting an Elizabeth or a
Mary Bennet, she sings at her task : an April
sun shines on the desired and the undesired.
All is light, clean, courtly, and everything she
says is interesting because she says it.   Johnson,
speaking in one of his most dignified passages
of Garrick's death, refers to it as an event that
had impoverished the public stock of harmless
pleasure, and Miss Austen's glory is similar.
Like Garrick, she has increased the gaiety of
her nation.   This, it seems to me, is what is to
be said of her; the first feeling one has when
one closes one of her novels is gratitude to the
author who has pleased so much.   Doubtless
she does more than arouse pleasurable sensations, she does more than cajole the reader into
good temper with himself.   Every one who
pleases us justly must do more while he pleases;
he must waken our judgment, he must excite
our fancy, he must appeal, if it is only on occasion, to our emotions.   All this we find, and could

not avoid finding, accomplished in 'Pride and
Prejudice,' or 'Mansfield Park,' and besides this,
as Miss Austen's admirers will tell us, we are
presented with an interesting comment upon
the social history of the times. For all that, we
think of these things with an effort, and when
we ask ourselves what Miss Austen has done
for us, we must reply, if our answer is to be
candid—She has produced delight.

Her singularity is not that she has done this,
but that in our judgment of her we think of it
first. The effect of every considerable author
must be something similar, he must please or
he will not be read. To increase our knowledge
of life, to enlarge our sympathies, to teach us,
as Wordsworth's claim runs, "to see, to think,
and to feel," is in a very real sense to increase
our happiness. Only with any author of weight
we think of a hundred things before we think
of this ; our debt to him is so large, the benefits
he has conferred so great that we think of them
with scarce a thought for their inevitable result.
With Miss Austen it is different : no critical
analysis will reveal anything in her that is not
summed up for good in the one word delightful,
and no critical analysis can deprive her novels

of their right to the adjective. To insist on her
separate excellences would be misleading ; they
are many, but they are not the cause of her
charm. If we consider her knowledge of character, and especially of feminine character, we
shall see that her achievement even here would
not of itself entitle her to a place of very high
distinction. From the play of 'Othello' alone
one learns six times more of what it is important
to know about woman, than from the whole six
of her novels. 'The Antiquary' tells us more
of what is essential in human character than all
she has left. If it is stated that she has enlarged
our sympathies, it must be answered those only
of people naturally sympathetic, and who are
thus protected from the hardening effect of her
constant stream of gentle cynicism.   There
is nothing in what she says to which on the
score of cynicism objection can be taken. She
does not over-emphasize the poor side of
humanity. On the contrary, she seldom speaks
of it with the severity it deserves, but she never
allows us to lose sight of it. She has no
ardours which induce her for a moment to
forget exceptions, and if after reading 'Emma'
a man naturally sympathetic will look more

charitably on the Miss Bates's of country towns, a spirit not " finely touched " will not be led by the perusal of her novels to " fine issues." Judged as those of a humane writer, the effect of her books is not great. For the purpose of expanding a cold or selfish nature, Thackeray's 'Roundabout Papers' have more potency than everything she wrote; it is doubtful if Marianne Dashwood herself would have found a tear for the sorrows of her fellow characters.

But it is useless to run over a catalogue of single virtues. Miss Austen is the mistress of a pretty school, she is not a master to whom any one would turn to learn about life. To proceed with her as we proceed with the great authors, by summing up in detail what has been done, would not be to establish but to minimize her excellence. To establish that we have to travel by another road; we have to start by stating what generally forms the conclusion of praise, and as to the justice of which as regards her there can be no possible doubt. There can be, it is necessary to insist on it, no possible doubt that she has contributed to our happiness, or rather those who praise Miss Austen can allow of no doubt about it, for unless the pro-

position be admitted at the outset their case is
gone. Fortunately the proposition, when carefully considered, is one to which no one is likely
to take exception. It does not imply that every
one who reads her novels is necessarily delighted ;
it cannot be expected to imply what would
amount to a contradiction of fact. A maid-
servant, for instance, will probably not indulge
in any excessive hilarity at the inanity of Mrs.
Bennet, or the preposterousness of Mr. Collins.
The factory ·worker, the shop assistant, the
soldier, the sailor, the marine, will concur in
thinking Miss Austen dull ; as representatives
of the classes to which they belong, they will
miss the spice of "moving accidents;" a
" milliner of Bath " will find little of interest in
' Northanger Abbey.' Miss Austen's appeal, it
may be granted, is to a comparatively limited
number, to a class sufficiently educated to per-
ceive the fine shade of her distinctions, and to
be pleased with stories not such as would be
told by the mere teller of tales.

From this limited audience some deductions
have to be made. There are some, not I think
many, who, though competent, fail to appreciate
her. Her peculiar, light, sarcastic comment on

almost everything that came into her range of vision, produces an irritating effect upon those who, while able to understand satire when dignified by anger, have no patience with her habit, of saying a trifle more than she means, and of sacrificing the strict letter of fact to her desire to excite the intelligence. Satire, at its best, is nothing else than angry truth, but she, when most satirical, is often but playing with ideas.

" Between Barton and Delaford," she writes, concluding 'Sense and Sensibility,' "there was that constant communication which strong family affection would naturally dictate; and among the merits and the happiness of Elinor and Marianne, let it not be ranked as the least considerable, that, though sisters, and living almost within sight of each other, they could live without disagreement between themselves, or producing coolness between their husbands."

Those who take such passages seriously, and refuse to see that this is but the pinch of salt to allow the reader to find flavour at the end, are bound to be disappointed with them, to find in them something a little flippant, a little silly. Then again from that portion of the educated class which is left to her, from that portion, which, capable of seriousness, does not always choose to be serious, another deduction must be made.

Among young people, however cultivated, the
majority will not be found her admirers. Her
mundane view of affairs, her real interest in income,
dress, manner, habit, position, alienates at once
all those whose notions are youthfully romantic.
Marianne is the only one of her characters who
will be easily understood by youth, and her
treatment of her will not seem, and perhaps it
is well that it should not seem, to be right. The
things which are admired in youth, are not
those with which Miss Austen has concern. A
young girl may be interested in dress, may be
interested in the income or position of her lover,
but this is in actual practice, and even in actual
practice she will despise herself for doing so.
Youth sees the large things in life, sees them
too exclusively perhaps, and is apt to write
nonsense about them, but still sees them,
whereas it was at the little things that Miss
Austen looked. There comes a time when it
is tonic to see matters in proportion, but it does
not come in the school-room ; one has read a
great number of books before one learns to value
the social sense of the author of ' Pride and Prejudice.' On the composition of her public it is
not necessary to say more, but it may be

suggested that the majority is male, educated women as a rule having a greater tendency to consistent seriousness than is compatible with a genuine love of intelligence at play. If it is so, and such remarks as have been made, and still more the quantity of remarks that have not been made, by her female critics go to show that so it is, it is an instance of the oddity of literary fates that woman's lightest painter, and certainly not her worst, should find the smaller portion of her audience among her own sex.

About the enthusiasm of that audience there is no question—an enthusiasm moreover which is reasoned and discriminating. Exaggerated claims are occasionally made for her work, but these are the freaks of jaded critics, anxious possibly to say something new on an exhausted subject, amusing themselves perhaps, by setting out to prove a little more than they think capable of proof, or attempting to supply new justification for an admiration for which the old justification was sufficient. Such claims are not advanced by the bulk of her public. It is remarkable that, the admiration she excites being so great, so much discrimination should be shown by her admirers. Yet, so it is. Great is the admiration she has excited, and great is the discrimination with which she is admired. The literary class, as a whole, is bound to have sobriety in its judgments, and Miss Austen's books are especially those to delight the literary class.

To the literary class—and the phrase will be understood to include many who have never printed a line—there is no virtue more attractive than that of style. If it is not true that every workman takes pleasure in doing his work well, at least he likes to see it well done. When Harry of Monmouth pays his tribute to the character of Hotspur, he praises him for doing excellently what he himself did. He had seen him, he says, "witching the world with noble horsemanship." And as a rider loves a good rider in spite of every inducement to the contrary, so the dealers in phrases love one who turns her phrases with skill. The politician, the lawyer, the cleric, the author, all occupy their lives in some kind of talk, they depend for their effect upon their mastery of words ; so also the member of any profession who aspires to distinction in it or in society, soon learns how much depends upon how he says a thing. There is no educated man who is blind to the importance of the manner in which he delivers himself of his matter, to the importance of style. He may not play the game perfectly, but he will be delighted whenever he sees it perfectly played, a reflection uttered, a comment passed in the most fitting form possible. And here he will find that Miss Austen abundantly satisfies him. Her style does every justice to her matter, she excels in the beauty of her workmanship, in the fitness of her language, in the skill with which she clothes her thoughts in sentences turned without apparent effort, and faultlessly neat.

Her manner and method are as perfect; she knows exactly when she has said enough, where the reader may be safely left to supply the necessary comment; and she knows when it is essential that she should say something, where the aid of her sensitive intelligence is wanted. No one knew better how to introduce an incident. The arrival of Bingley in 'Pride and Prejudice' shows this side of her art in perfection. There everything is trifling, ordinary, commonplace. A young man pays a call, and the reader's attention is caught. To any incident, however innocent, Miss Austen possessed

the power of lending a transitory importance,
as she also possessed the much rarer power of
touching a grave incident so lightly as to bring
it into tone with its surroundings. 'Pride and
Prejudice,' for example, is a story in which
gravity would be out of place. The heroine's
sister Lydia is a girl of sixteen or seventeen,
and about the middle of the book a young
scamp, by name Wickham, takes it into his
head to run off with her. Put in plain English,
in a novel .dealing with the girlish loves of a
family of girls, we find ourselves concerned with
a story of abduction. Here was an opportunity
for a moralist, and how few would have missed
it; one trembles to think what might not have
been said. In how many hands would 'Pride
and Prejudice,' beginning as a comedy, have
ended brightly? But Miss Austen means it to
end so; she feels instinctively that the incident
is not light enough for its surroundings, and she
exhausts the resources of her art to reduce its
importance. Lydia is giddy, she tells us that
clearly; Wickham is an impudent scamp, she
does not conceal his rascality, but she forces his
impudence so delightfully to the front that we
cannot choose but laugh. "I admire all my

U

three sons-in-law highly," says Mr. Bennet; and adds, "Wickham, perhaps, is my favourite." One sees the sense of this satire; and if Lydia's marriage to Wickham is only the " cobbling " of an awkward blunder, and we are a trifle surprised that the family should acquiesce in it as gaily as they do, we soon forget that in watching the absurd enthusiasm of Mrs. Bennet. This adventure of a couple of madcaps becomes ridiculous enough, and we find ourselves laughing at it without being able to reproach Miss Austen with the least indelicacy, the least fault in taste. What a charming humour, what fineness of handling was necessary before such a result could be achieved, and this is due to her manner, to her quick perception of the incongruous, to her power of saying what ought, and no more than what ought, to be said. It is a merit which endears her to those whose reading is extensive, and who are accustomed to find incidents mismanaged or run to death, the right thing not said, or not what is right in the particular place, and the wrong tone often perversely taken.

The good sense and good taste of Miss Austen are everywhere, and so everywhere is

her wit. Most people start life in an attitude
of profound seriousness, with a strong individual
outlook: "I have lost my rattle," cry the per-
petually young, as if others were always thinking
of its loss; and to discover that the world was
not contrived for any person, or at all to favour
vanity, is to take a stride in serviceable age. But
the revulsion of feeling is often too sudden, and
laughter is resorted to, for Byron's reason, that
one "may not weep." There comes, of course,
the final stage, in the quaint language of high-
sounding philosophy, the reconciliation of oppo-
sites—a stage in which one is not violent on one
side or the other, and sees the extravagance of
excess. To have one's temper under command,
and yet to feel the promptings of indignation,
to be amused, and yet to appreciate that there
is more in folly than laughter can adequately
criticize, this is the usual mood of those to whom
books and experience have taught something.
It is a mood to be abandoned only on the pressure of some great occasion, and one which Miss
Austen, who touches little on great occasions,
exactly suits. *Castigat ridendo;* but we do not
hear the crack of the whip, and her laugh at
follies, which she knows will survive it, is not

very loud. There is a familiar story that a
Chinaman and a chimney-sweep, meeting in
Lincoln's Inn Fields, fell to laughing at each
other so heartily as to endanger their health
Miss Austen will not join in their hilarity, she
has seen many like them, and is aware that
neither a Chinaman nor a chimney-sweep is
ridiculous to himself. Nor do I think had she
lived two centuries earlier and seen Jews parad-
ing in yellow, or the fires which the constant
martyrs of England's versatile ecclesiasticism
lit, she would have been loud in her disgust.
Custom, she would say, if she had ever con-
descended to a generality, is firmly planted, let
us be content where it is too serious for our
smiles to let it pass.

Undoubtedly it was not a heroic attitude, it
was not even an attitude which was likely to
have much weight with the large bands of noisily
honest people who control the modern world.
Miss Austen hated avarice, and Molière has
done infinitely more than she has to make
avarice detestable. But for those who love the
truth, who desire to see the thing as it is, to be
grateful, in Mr. Kipling's phrase—and where
shall we find franker phrases than Mr. Kipling's?

—to "the God of things as they are," her attitude is the best.   There are few Harpagons in
existence.   Harpagon as a type—splendid caricature though he is—is a caricature.   Mr. and
Mrs. John Dashwood walk the streets every day,
and for all who take an artistic pleasure in hearing just what is true they are charming figures.
There is a whole volume of instruction in the
second chapter of 'Sense and Sensibility.'   By
his first marriage Mr. Henry Dashwood had a
son, John Dashwood; and by his second two
daughters.   Towards the close of his life, when
his children were grown up, he succeeded to a
great estate, entailed strictly however, much to
his chagrin, on his only son, who, by a "good"
marriage and the fortune of settlements, had
already far more money than his two sisters and
their mother.   The only hope of Mr. Henry
Dashwood was that he would survive long
enough to make provision out of the income
for his widow and children.

"But the fortune, which had been so tardy in
coming, was his only one twelvemonth.   He survived his uncle no longer; and ten thousand
pounds was all that remained for his widow and
daughters.   His son was sent for as soon as his

danger was known, and to him Mr. Dashwood recommended, with all the strength and urgency which illness could command, the interest of his mother-in-law and sisters."

In the furtherance of his dead father's wishes, Mr. John Dashwood, a man of six thousand a year, thinks "something must be done." At first his generosity extends to the idea of a free gift of a fiftieth part of his possessions, but declines on "neighbourly acts." The inimitable conversation, in the second chapter, which passes between him and his wife, in which his original proposal of three thousand pounds is reduced by the most natural steps to fifteen hundred, an annuity of a hundred, an occasional douceur of fifty, and finally to presents of fish and game "whenever they are in season," with the running fire of "to be sures," and "certainly nots," and the general atmosphere of virtuous concern, is as admirable a piece of irony as is to be found in the language. What could be finer than Mrs. John Dashwood's discovery that it was "the more unkind" of her father to saddle her mother with the payment of an annuity to some old servants, "because otherwise the money would have been entirely at her mother's disposal," or

that their own child had the more exclusive
claim on their fortune because he was an only
one? Making allowance for that slight heightening which is necessary for art, there is nothing
in the whole of the passage which could not
have passed any day between a rich man and
his wife on the subject of their poor relations.
And the charming thing about Miss Austen is
that she leaves the matter here. Mr. and Mrs.
John Dashwood are mean paltry people, and
whenever we catch a momentary glimpse of
them, we find them just the same, but with none
of their vices exaggerated, and with none of
their decent behaviour forgotten. Some authors,
when they have to deal with such people, can
never have done with them; in their hands they
become misers pure and simple, they plunge
into a career of blackness. A bad heart, they
seem to wish to tell us, leads to all manner of
badness; but does it—does it not happen otherwise as often as not? Dashwood is pleased to
hear of any good fortune falling the way of his
sisters, he has a windy sympathy for people in
misfortune in no way connected with him, as
a husband and a father he behaves with propriety. How much meanness is there in the

world which results in nothing worse than the negation of good, how pitiful are the characters of many who come to respected ends!

A study of manners, however fleeting, will go sometimes below the surface, and a novelist of character as clear-sighted and as truthful as Miss Austen has, like every traveller, however circumscribed the area of his journey, "a tale to tell." It is as easy to under-rate her service as it is to overvalue it. She "sweeps a room," but she performs her task so deftly and with such bright-eyed diligence that she makes "the action fine." On the other hand her achievement appears greater than it is, because in the nature of things it is insusceptible of imitation. It will hardly happen again that a writer of equal power will take quite so seriously the society in which he happens to be placed, or watch so lovingly its ways of habit. He will not see the same finality in its frightened compromises, its blunt and capricious ethics, its constant illogicalness. He will be less satisfied with the huge artificial fabric, with which men each century afresh pay tribute for security. The imagination of the new world will spread itself in two directions : in one, and it is perhaps the path which the best will choose, in a ceaseless didactic effort to bring social ordinances and feeling more in consonance with a morality ampler than rules express; in the other, in an effort to escape. The artist with the instinct of his art strong in him, will not come down, as Miss Austen came down, to meet his  time, where certain lines of conduct evoke an equally stereotyped approval or blame. He will hope, either by removing his scene to a past civilization, or by dealing only with those actions, passions, and dispositions which have no limit of place, to appeal to a judgment that is not conventional. He will escape from what is thought or said, to speak of what is, and because he does so his appeal will be lasting. For just as the Hindoo and the Italian are both impressed by the easy triumphs of Nature, and watch with equal wonder the growth of the leaf, or the myriad suns that peep through "the blanket of the dark," so the sorrows of Dido touch the heart of a Mormon, and the utilitarian who accepts Plato's dogma concerning poetry takes a pleasure, in spite of himself, in Shakespeare's noble lies.

THE END

THACKERAY: a Study. By Adolphus Alfred Jack. Crown 8vo. 3s. 6d.

Review of Reviews—"Always bright and interesting."

Cambridge Review—"We have read this volume with considerable interest and pleasure. It is full of good things."

Scotsman—"Will be read with interest by many."

Glasgow Herald—"Mr. Jack may be congratulated on this sound and sensible contribution to the literature of criticism."

St. James's Gazette—"A piece of careful, appreciative, and interesting work."

BY F. MARION CRAWFORD.

THE NOVEL: What it is. Portrait as Frontispiece. Pott 8vo. 3s.

Scotsman—"Every one who knows Mr. Crawford's work in fiction will read the book with a keen interest, and it may well appeal to a wider circle."

Glasgow Herald—"Full of admirable passages as to the history, character, and destiny of the novel as a literary instrument and an incidental moral force."

Leeds Mercury—"Deserves to be widely read in thoughtful circles. In brief compass, and with a felicity of thought as well as of phrase which is noteworthy, the nature, mission, scope, and characteristics of the novel as a force in present-day society are admirably discussed."

MACMILLAN AND CO., Ltd., LONDON.

BY RUDYARD KIPLING.

SOLDIER TALES. Containing "With the Main Guard," "The Drums of the Fore and Aft," "The Man who was," "Courting of Dinah Shadd," "Incarnation of Krishna Mulvaney," "Taking of Lungtungpen," "The Madness of Private Ortheris." With Head and Tail Pieces, and Twenty-one Page Illustrations by A. S. HARTRICK. Crown 8vo, Cloth gilt. Uniform with *Jungle Book. 6s.*

Daily News—" Mr. Kipling's stories of Mulvaney and Co. are as captivating at the tenth reading as at the first—as all stories of first-rate genius are."

THE SECOND JUNGLE BOOK. With Illustrations by J. LOCKWOOD KIPLING. Twenty-second Thousand.

Daily Telegraph—" The' appearance of *The Second Jungle Book* is a literary event of which no one will mistake the importance. Unlike most sequels, the various stories comprised in the new volume are at least equal to their predecessors."

THE JUNGLE BOOK. With Illustrations by J. L. KIPLING, W. H. DRAKE, and P. FRENZENY. Thirtieth Thousand. Crown 8vo. 6s.

Athenæum—" We tender our sincere thanks to Mr. Kipling for the hour of pure and unadulterated enjoyment which he has given us, and many another reader, by this inimitable *Jungle Book*."

Punch—"'Æsop's Fables and dear old Brer Fox and Co.,' observes the Baron sagely, ' may have suggested to the fanciful genius of Rudyard Kipling the delightful idea, carried out in the most fascinating style, of *The Jungle Book.*'"

WEE WILLIE WINKIE and other Stories. Crown 8vo. 6s.

SOLDIERS THREE and other Stories. Crown 8vo. 6s.

St. James's Gazette—" In these, as the faithful are aware, is contained some of Mr. Kipling's very finest work."

Globe—" Containing some of the best of his highly vivid work."

PLAIN TALES FROM THE HILLS. Thirty-first Thousand. Crown 8vo. 6s.

Saturday Review—" Mr. Kipling knows and appreciates the English in India, and is a born story-teller and a man of humour into the bargain. . . . It would be hard to find better reading."

Glasgow Herald—" Character, situation, incident, humour, pathos, tragic force, are all in abundance; words alone are at a minimum. Of course these are 'plain' tales—lightning-flash tales. A gleam, and there the whole tragedy or comedy is before you—elaborate it for yourself afterwards."

THE LIGHT THAT FAILED. Rewritten and considerably enlarged. Twentieth Thousand. Crown 8vo. 6s.

Academy—"Whatever else be true of Mr. Kipling, it is the first truth about him that he has power, real intrinsic power. . . . Mr. Kipling's work has innumerable good qualities."

Manchester Courier—" The story is a brilliant one and full of vivid interest."

LIFE'S HANDICAP. Being Stories of Mine Own People. Twenty-third Thousand. Crown 8vo. 6s.

Black and White—" *Life's Handicap* contains much of the best work hitherto accomplished by the author, and, taken as a whole, is a complete advance upon its predecessors."

Observer—" The stories are as good as ever, and are quite as well told. . . . *Life's Handicap* is a volume that can be read with pleasure and interest under almost any circumstances."

MANY INVENTIONS. Twentieth Thousand. Crown 8vo. 6s.

Pall Mall Gazette—" The completest book that Mr. Kipling has yet given us in workmanship, the weightiest and most humane in breadth of view. . . . It can only be regarded as a fresh landmark in the progression of his genius."

National Observer—" The book is one for all Mr. Kipling's admirers to rejoice in —some for this, and some for that, and not a few for well-nigh everything it contains."

MACMILLAN AND CO., LTD., LONDON.